EVIDENCE-BASED PREVENTION

Other Books in the Prevention Practice Kit

Katherine Raczynski: *To Kevin*

Michael Waldo: *This book is gratefully dedicated to those who evaluate and promote best practices in prevention.*

Jonathan Schwartz: *To my wonderful and supportive wife Marie and my amazing children Mazelle and Jayvin.*

Arthur Horne: *To Bob Conyne. Thanks for the 3+ decades of professional engagement and friendship.*

EVIDENCE-BASED PREVENTION

KATHERINE RACZYNSKI
University of Georgia

MICHAEL WALDO
New Mexico State University

JONATHAN P. SCHWARTZ
University of Houston

ARTHUR M. HORNE
University of Georgia

Los Angeles | London | New Delhi
Singapore | Washington DC

Los Angeles | London | New Delhi
Singapore | Washington DC

FOR INFORMATION:

SAGE Publications, Inc.
2455 Teller Road
Thousand Oaks, California 91320
E-mail: order@sagepub.com

SAGE Publications Ltd.
1 Oliver's Yard
55 City Road
London EC1Y 1SP
United Kingdom

SAGE Publications India Pvt. Ltd.
B 1/I 1 Mohan Cooperative Industrial Area
Mathura Road, New Delhi 110 044
India

SAGE Publications Asia-Pacific Pte. Ltd.
3 Church Street
#10-04 Samsung Hub
Singapore 049483

Acquisitions Editor: Kassie Graves
Editorial Assistant: Elizabeth Luizzi
Production Editor: Brittany Bauhaus
Copy Editor: QuADS Prepress (P) Ltd.
Typesetter: C&M Digitals (P) Ltd.
Proofreader: Jeff Bryant
Indexer: Diggs Publication Services, Inc.
Cover Designer: Glenn Vogel
Marketing Manager: Lisa Sheldon Brown
Permissions Editor: Adele Hutchinson

Copyright © 2013 by SAGE Publications, Inc.

Printed in the United States of America

Library of Congress Cataloging-in-Publication Data

Evidence-based prevention / editors, Katherine Raczynski . . . [et al.].

p. cm. — (Prevention practice kit)
Includes bibliographical references and index.

ISBN 978-1-4522-5800-3 (pbk.)

1. Preventive mental health services. 2. Evidence-based medicine. I. Raczynski, Katherine A.

RA790.E935 2013
362.2'0425—dc23   2012040375

This book is printed on acid-free paper.

12 13 14 15 16 10 9 8 7 6 5 4 3 2 1

Brief Contents _____

Detailed Contents _____

Acknowledgments____

We want to thank Robert Conyne for providing the leadership to pull this important work together. And we want to thank our remarkable coauthors, whose knowledge, creativity, persistence, and patience have been unfailing protective factors. Thank you!

Introduction _____

Ms. Rodriguez has just been hired as a counselor at North Shoals High School. She is fresh out of graduate school and is brimming with enthusiasm. One of her priorities is to implement a parenting program to help prevent teen drug use. She attended a professional school counselors' conference over the summer and purchased a manual for the program she wishes to implement. When she discussed her plan with the school principal, he tells her that he is generally in favor of the program, but that he would like for her to research the program to make sure that it is evidence based. What does that mean and where should Ms. Rodriguez begin?

Mr. Moore is a therapist at a residential treatment program for troubled youth. He wants to start a new group counseling program for the prevention of dating violence. His director allows him to move forward with the program but asks him to collect evidence on the effectiveness of the program and to report back with results in 6 months. What types of evidence should Mr. Moore collect? How should he go about collecting it?

The term *evidence based* has recently become somewhat of a buzzword. Counselors, psychologists, and mental health workers in schools, government agencies, community settings, and in private practice are increasingly expected to select evidence-based programs and treatments and to document the effectiveness of the care they provide. In school, government, and community settings, mental health workers have seen demands for the use of evidence-based programs by funding agencies. For example, in Oregon, it is required by law that 75% of state-funded mental health and substance abuse services be identified as evidence based (Rieckmann, Bergmann, & Rasplica, 2011). It seems likely that this trend of linking state dollars to evidence-based care will expand to other states as well. For those working in public schools, the political winds that have brought an increased emphasis on accountability and data-driven decision making have also placed demands on counselors to provide evidence-based practice and to produce data indicating the types of results one's efforts have generated. The No Child Left Behind Act and the Individuals with Disabilities Act both stipulate that school-based personnel must select interventions that are scientific and research based (Raines, 2008, p. 8). Finally, mental health workers who receive payment through clients' insurance are finding more and more restrictions placed on the type of care that is covered. Therapists and psychologists may find that given a particular diagnosis, only a small list of evidence-based treatments are approved for reimbursement.

One of the primary benefits of the shift toward evidence-based practice is the ability to compare different approaches to prevention. A goal of the evidence-based movement is to offer practitioners objective information regarding which programs have demonstrated particular desirable benefits and what the costs of those programs are. Comparing approaches also enables practitioners to choose those that best fit the needs and circumstances of the people they want to help. Different prevention approaches may fit different populations because of cultural variables, age, income, education, social contexts, marital status, sexual orientation, settings, schedules, and a wide variety of other factors. For example, a group intervention to improve relationship skills that works well in a college residence hall could be ineffective, counterproductive, or even impossible, working with rural families. Or a preventive intervention offered via the web that is helpful to rural families may be very ineffective for low-income families who do not have ready access to computers. If prevention practitioners have information regarding the effectiveness of different prevention approaches, they are in a better position to choose the approach that is most appropriate for their participants.

Perhaps most important, examining evidence on effectiveness enables practitioners to identify prevention strategies that don't work or that may even make problems worse. For example, there are two well-intended prevention programs for youth that have been shown to not only not achieve their goals but to have an opposite impact. The Drug Abuse Resistance Education program (D.A.R.E.) is intended to prevent youth's experimentation with substance use, and the "Scared Straight" program is intended to prevent youth's involvement in criminal behavior. Careful evaluation of these preventive interventions has revealed worse outcomes for the youth involved in them (West & O'Neal, 2004). Based on research outcomes, participants in the D.A.R.E. program are more, rather than less, likely to experiment with drugs. Youth who participated in the "Scared Straight" program are more, rather than less, likely to admire a criminal lifestyle (Petrosino, Turpin-Petrosino, & Finckenauer, 2000). These findings demonstrate that preventive interventions can be for "better or worse" (Cohen, 1994). We even know that some approaches may cause additional or unintended consequences. In medicine, a treatment that results in developing an illness or problem is referred to as "iatrogenic"—medically caused. As we examine programs, it is especially important to be able to identify situations where problems become exacerbated rather than improved. We are called as psychologists, counselors, and mental health workers to "above all, do no harm" (American Counseling Association, 2005); therefore, it is critical that we know when preventive interventions may produce deleterious outcomes.

However, substantial criticism has also been directed at the movement toward evidence-based practices and programs. Psychologists have argued that the randomized controlled trials (RCTs) that are often used to establish evidence-based practices have shortcomings and that other programs may be just as effective (e.g., Messer, 2004). For example, Westen (2006) calls into question the generalizability of the results of psychotherapy RCTs by arguing that (a) participants in RCTs are dissimilar to typical patients and (b) the treatments that are evaluated in RCTs are dissimilar to the types of treatments practiced in the community. He states that restrictive exclusion criteria disqualifies a substantial number of participants in RCTs—for example, those who have symptoms of more than one disorder—but that these excluded participants may represent a substantial portion of individuals seeking treatment. Furthermore, participants in RCTs may not adequately represent diverse populations (e.g., Sue & Zane, 2006). To the extent that participants in RCTs do not represent the targeted population, the results of the trial may not generalize to the individuals who will participate in the program in practice.

Westen (2006) also states that certain types of programs are more likely to be evaluated with RCTs and that these tested programs are not adequately representative of the treatment approaches employed in practice. He argues that researchers may select programs to evaluate based on practical questions such as What is likely to get funded? What practices could easily be turned into a manualized program? What programs are brief enough to be easily tested? Therefore, the programs that undergo evaluation may be the programs that are most suited to being evaluated and not necessarily those that are the most impactful. Furthermore, because programs are often tested against placebos instead of other widely used approaches, clinicians may not have enough information to be convinced that the tested approach is superior to their current practices. Westen states, "I cannot remember the last time I read the results of an RCT and was impressed that the average patient was better off than the average patient in my practice" (p. 169).

A further area of contention surrounding evidence-based practices involves the use of treatment manuals. Following a highly detailed program manual lends the appearance of objectivity to an evaluation and allows for a program to be implemented in a similar way in other settings. However, some argue that manualized programs are no better than nonmanualized programs and that it is not possible to encapsulate the effective ingredients of a psychological intervention in a manual (Duncan & Miller, 2006). One argument against manualization pertains to what is seen as a de-emphasis on the therapeutic relationship, as described in the following quotation:

> The idea of making psychological interventions dummy-proof has a certain seductive appeal, where the users—the client and the therapist—are basically irrelevant. This product view of therapy is perhaps the most vacuous aspect of manualization because the treatment itself accounts for so little of outcome variance, whereas the client and the therapist, and their relationship, account for so much. (Duncan & Miller, 2006, p. 145)

There is also some evidence to suggest that some aspects of the therapeutic relationship may suffer as therapists change their behaviors to adhere to a treatment manual. For example, Henry, Strupp, Butler, Schacht, and Binder (1993) state that "therapists often report feeling that their spontaneity and intuition are curtailed, whereas patients sometimes feel 'subjected' to a treatment in a manner that overlooks their individual needs" (p. 438).

So what are we to think of this push for evidence-based practice and programs? Should we rejoice at the prospect of having research at our fingertips to inform and improve our practice as mental health professionals? Will the overall quality of care advance over time as effective programs make the grade and ineffective programs are exposed? Or will counselors and psychologists be forced to robotically adhere to proscriptive programs with no room for clinical judgment and expertise? Will innovation be stifled as new (and therefore necessarily) unproven approaches are denied access to funding? And who gets to decide what counts as evidence anyway?

The debate over evidence-based programs is a contentious one. In this book, we hope to shed light on multiple sides of the issue while retaining a balanced perspective. Most important, we hope to answer the types of questions that may be most pertinent to counselors, psychologists, and other mental health workers who are engaged in prevention and interested in understanding evidence-based programs. The questions addressed in this monograph include the following:

- What does it mean for a program to be evidence based?
- How should I go about selecting an evidence-based program?
- How do I know if evidence is trustworthy?
- How do I gather evidence to evaluate my own prevention program?

In Chapter 1, we discuss several definitions of evidence-based practice and the common components of these definitions: best research evidence, clinical expertise, and client/patient values and preferences. While the definition and components of evidence-based practice are widely accepted, how these components are prioritized has been an issue of debate.

In Chapter 2, we provide a broad overview of common considerations for evaluating the quality and trustworthiness of prevention research. These considerations include the types of data collected, the study design employed, and the steps taken to minimize threats to internal and external validity. We discuss the importance of collecting evaluation evidence over multiple research studies to obtain a more comprehensive assessment of the quality of the prevention program.

In Chapter 3, we present criteria for evidence-based practice and programs. We discuss common features of effective prevention programs, including principles related to program characteristics, matching the program with the targeted population, and implementation and evaluation of prevention programs. We provide an overview of the Society for Prevention Research criteria for designating a prevention program as efficacious, effective, and ready for dissemination. We also discuss the importance of matching evidence-based prevention to sound theory and provide a classification scheme for organizing research evidence.

In Chapter 4, we focus on selecting and implementing evidence-based programs. We describe several available registries of prevention programs and other methods for identifying promising programs. Furthermore, we summarize the process of matching your own circumstances and needs to a program that addresses those needs and implementing and evaluating a prevention program. In this section, we also discuss issues pertaining to the translation of evidence-based programs. For instance, if you have selected a prevention program with solid evidence demonstrating its effectiveness in a mostly suburban white population, how might you adapt the program to be more appropriate for a rural Hispanic population or an inner-city impoverished community?

Our goals for this book are as follows. We wish to shed light on some of the debate and controversy regarding evidence-based programs, so that readers will be able to better navigate the waters surrounding this important and emerging topic. We want readers to have confidence in locating promising prevention programs and assessing the quality of the evidence base that is presented, and we want readers to be able to develop a plan for implementing and evaluating their own prevention programs. It is an exciting time to be practicing prevention, and we hope that quality of care will be improved as researchers and practitioners engage in a more careful evaluation of evidence supporting prevention programs.

Before continuing, we wish to review some basic information pertaining to prevention efforts to help frame our discussion of evidence-based prevention. For a more comprehensive overview of prevention in general, please see the first book in this Toolkit, *Prevention in Psychology: An Introduction to the Prevention Practice Kit* (Conyne, Horne, & Raczynski, 2012).

Prevention has been conceptualized as falling along a continuum of activities focused on improving mental health and well-being. The Institute of Medicine (IOM; O'Connell, Boat, & Warner, 2009) defined this continuum as being made up of four levels: (1) mental health promotion, (2) prevention, (3) treatment, and (4) maintenance. *Mental health promotion* refers to efforts to enhance well-being, such as activities that foster resiliency, a sense of purpose and competence, positive self-esteem, and social connectedness. *Prevention* refers to efforts to stop the onset of mental health problems. *Treatment* refers to identifying individuals with mental health problems and providing standard remediation. *Maintenance* refers to appropriate aftercare (e.g., rehabilitation) and efforts to promote long-term adherence to treatment, with the goal of reduction of relapse.

Prevention efforts have further been divided into several types. Multiple classification schemes for prevention efforts have been developed; in this monograph, we employ two popular conceptualizations forwarded by

Gordon (1987) and Caplan (1964). Gordon's (1987) typology defines three levels of prevention of increasing intensity: (1) universal, (2) selective, and (3) indicated. This classification system considers a risk–benefit balance that evaluates the risk of the disorder based on the characteristics of the intended audience along with the costs and benefits of the prevention effort. As efforts become more intensive, they often become more costly, both in terms of the resources needed to carry out the intervention and the amount of time and effort required by participants. Therefore, prevention efforts that are more extensive and demanding may only be appropriate for individuals at elevated risk.

Universal prevention involves efforts that benefit the entire population regardless of their level of risk for developing the targeted disorder or problem. For example, all individuals could benefit from accurate information pertaining to ways to reduce stress in their lives or training to develop more effective social interaction skills related to conflict resolution. In medical application terms, we might think of this as the inclusion of fluoride in public water systems; all people receive the prevention program. *Selective* prevention efforts are targeted at individuals with elevated risk. A selective prevention program may involve a group counseling series for new parents on how to handle the stress of adjusting to life with a new baby or a program may be developed for students whose parents are engaged in separation or divorce. In medical application terms, we may consider people who have a history of family heart disease being on an aspirin regimen; it is not recommended for all people, but it may be important for those who have been identified as at elevated risk of heart disease. *Indicated* preventions are aimed at those at high risk. They may include multipronged efforts (i.e., working individually and with the families of soldiers with wartime injuries), and these efforts may be of longer duration than other levels of prevention. Another example may be with students who have missed a significant number of school days, have a poor academic record, and are known to be hanging out with a group of peers who have been in legal trouble. Especially as prevention efforts become more costly, evidence supporting the positive impact of a particular program with regard to its intended benefits is invaluable. In medical application terms, we may consider people who have had a heart attack who then are engaged in a coronary support group effort; they have experienced a severe problem, and a major support program, while expensive, is justified to prevent further difficulties in the future.

Caplan (1964) developed another popular classification scheme for categorizing types of prevention efforts within the mental health field. This conceptualization includes three levels of prevention: (1) primary, (2) secondary, and (3) tertiary. *Primary* prevention involves preventing new occurrences of a disorder, such as a substance abuse prevention program aimed at preventing adolescents from trying drugs. *Secondary* prevention is concerned with reducing the prevalence of existing cases of a disorder, such as by identifying adolescents who are abusing drugs and providing treatment. *Tertiary* prevention involves reducing the community-level consequences of existing illness, such as by providing supports for individuals who have been treated for substance abuse to reenter the labor force.

Activity

The debate over evidence-based practices and programs has been dubbed a "culture war" between those who approach psychology from more scientific and more humanistic viewpoints, often with researchers on one side of the divide and practitioners on the other (Messer, 2004). Based on the information provided above and your own experiences, consider the following questions.

- What do you see as the primary benefits of evidence-based prevention?
- What do you see as potential problems with evidence-based prevention?
- To what extent do you believe that the impact of prevention programs and practices can be objectively studied?
- If you were asked to choose a prevention program to implement in your community, how would you go about making your selection? What types of evidence would you find most compelling?

Definitions and Components of Evidence-Based Practice and Programs

1

The IOM and the American Psychological Association (APA) have both adopted similar definitions of evidence-based practice. The IOM, in a definition adapted from Sackett, Straus, Richardson, Rosenberg, and Haynes (2000), states the following:

> *Evidence-based practice* is the integration of best research evidence with clinical expertise and patient values. *Best research evidence* refers to clinically relevant research, often from the basic health and medical sciences, but especially from patient centered clinical research into the accuracy and precision of diagnostic tests (including the clinical examination); the power of prognostic markers; and the efficacy and safety of therapeutic, rehabilitative, and preventive regimens. *Clinical expertise* means the ability to use clinical skills and past experience to rapidly identify each patient's unique health state and diagnosis, individual risks and benefits of potential interventions, and personal values and expectations. *Patient values* refers to the unique preferences, concerns, and expectations that each patient brings to a clinical encounter and that must be integrated into clinical decisions if they are to serve the patient. (p. 147)

The APA further adapted this definition to more specifically address evidence-based practice in psychology. A policy statement on evidence-based practice adopted in 2005 states the following:

> Evidence-based practice in psychology (EBPP) is the integration of the best available research with clinical expertise in the context of patient characteristics, culture, and preferences. . . . The purpose of EBPP is to promote effective psychological practice and enhance public health by

applying empirically supported principles of psychological assessment, case formulation, therapeutic relationship, and intervention. (APA, 2005, p. 1)

These definitions share three key components: best research evidence, clinical expertise, and patient characteristics, values, and preferences. We will explore each of these components in turn.

Best Research Evidence

According to the APA policy statement on evidence-based practice in psychology, "Best research evidence refers to scientific results related to intervention strategies, assessment, clinical problems, and patient populations in laboratory and field settings as well as to clinically relevant results of basic research in psychology and related fields" (APA, 2005, p. 1). As the previous statement implies, multiple types of research evidence may be used to describe psychological practice. These types of evidence include efficacy, effectiveness, cost-effectiveness, cost–benefit, epidemiological, and treatment utilization (APA Presidential Task Force on Evidence-Based Practice, 2006). For example, a program may be deemed efficacious but not cost-effective. Types of evidence pertaining to efficacy, effectiveness, and cost-effectiveness are briefly summarized below.

Types of Evidence

Efficacy. *Efficacy* refers to the positive effects of a program that has been implemented under optimal circumstances. For example, consider a university researcher who has just developed a parenting program for the families of youths who have been adjudicated through the juvenile court system. The researcher is highly invested in the outcome of the study and will work hard to help ensure a high quality program. She may facilitate all of the group sessions herself or ensure that other facilitators are highly qualified and trained. She may spend extra time working with judges to make sure that they really understand which types of young people meet the criteria to be recommended into the program. An efficacious program is one that demonstrates benefits to participants under this type of optimal delivery.

Effectiveness. It is understandable that researchers will want to make sure that their programs are implemented in a high-quality manner. However, real-world conditions are not always ideal. For example, the staff members who may be implementing the program under day-to-day conditions may be juggling multiple other responsibilities. They may not have the same amount of time to devote to training and communication about the program. *Effectiveness* refers to the beneficial outcomes of a program implemented under more real-world circumstances. How well does the program work when regular staff members (i.e., court-appointed social workers or counselors), as opposed to outside researchers, facilitate the program? Effectiveness studies often focus on measuring the quality of implementation under these more naturalistic circumstances.

Cost-Effectiveness and Cost–Benefit. Cost-effectiveness and cost–benefit analyses are concerned with the benefits of a program relative to its cost, including financial costs and other impacts such as side effects. Benefits may take many forms. In the case of the parenting program, possible benefits include the reduction in human suffering (e.g., significant improvement in parent–child relationship), improved academic outcomes (e.g., greater school attendance, fewer discipline incidents, higher grades), and reduced cost to the juvenile court system. For instance, the parenting program may initially cost more than standard probation, but if rates of recidivism drop, the overall cost to the court may be reduced. Cost-effectiveness analyses help define the relative costs and benefits of implementing the program in the real world.

Psychologists, counselors, social workers, and other mental health workers should evaluate the nature of evidence across multiple levels of evidence, if available. Ideally, a well-supported program will have been evaluated and will have demonstrated benefits at more than one level. As mentioned in the introduction, preventive efforts at the *selective* and *indicated* level may be quite extensive, involved, and long-lasting. Before committing to a program that may be resource intensive, it is helpful to consider the following questions in light of the research evidence:

- What benefits have been demonstrated?
- Are the demonstrated benefits sufficiently connected to the intended goals of the program? For example, consider a program that is intended to prevent high school dropout. Is evidence that the program increases school connectedness enough to convince you of its value as a dropout prevention program without any other evidence that participants in the program were less likely to drop out of school?
- Has the program been shown to produce benefits when implemented in naturalistic settings?
- What are the costs of the program? Do these costs outweigh the benefits?

The Society for Prevention Research developed a comprehensive set of standards delineating the extent of evidence needed for a program to be considered (a) efficacious, (b) effective, and (c) ready for dissemination. The standards are described in Chapter 2.

Design of the Research Study

Another aspect of research evidence pertains to the design of the research study. A research study may produce impressive evidence of the benefits of a program, but if the design of the study is flawed, the results may not be trust-worthy. The APA Presidential Task Force on Evidence-Based Practice (2006) lists a variety of research designs that may contribute to evidence-based prac-tice, including the following:

- Clinical observation
- Qualitative research
- Systematic case studies
- Single-case experimental design
- Public health and ethnographic research
- Process–outcome studies
- Effectiveness research
- Randomized controlled trials
- Meta-analysis

There is a wealth of available information pertaining to research design, and it is beyond the scope of this work to provide a comprehensive overview of the topic. In this section, we will highlight just one research design, the randomized controlled design. This research design is particularly relevant to a discussion of evidence-based practice because it allows for a systematic evaluation of a program's impact.

Randomized Controlled Trials. RCTs have been deemed "the gold stan-dard" of research designs when it comes to producing evidence of the impact of a practice or program. According to IOM (O'Connell et al., 2009), "A well-conducted randomized trial is a high-precision instrument that leads to causal statements about a program's effect so that one can be assured that any observed differences are due to the different interven-tions and not some other factor" (p. 264). What makes RCTs a "high-precision instrument"? We believe that it is the ability to rule out competing explanations for the results of the evaluation. One way that this is accomplished is through assignment of participants to treatment and control groups.

Consider a prevention program designed to prevent abusive dating relation-ships on a college campus. The program consists of five 1-hour psychoeduca-tional group sessions held over the course of 5 weeks. One way to evaluate the impact of the program would be to ask the participants to rate their knowledge of and attitudes toward dating abuse before and after the intervention. However, without a comparison group that did not receive the intervention, it may be difficult to attribute any changes to the impact of the intervention as opposed to other factors. External factors may influence attitudes on dating abuse, for example, a high-profile event may take place that shines a spotlight on dating abuse (e.g., the arrest of a celebrity for harming a romantic partner). Any number of events that have nothing to do with the intervention may influ-ence how participants respond on the outcome measure. Even the normal growth and development that occurs with the passing of time can affect how participants respond. One purpose of a control group is to measure what changes have occurred as a result of external factors.

However, just having a control group is not enough to ensure that an accurate comparison can be drawn with the outcomes of the treatment group. Randomization is also crucial. Participants must be randomly assigned into groups to ensure that the composition of the groups is roughly equivalent in terms of relevant observed and unobserved characteristics. Observed characteristics may include sex, race/ethnicity, and initial status on the construct of interest (e.g., pretest attitudes regarding dating abuse). Unobserved characteristics may also play a role in influencing how participants respond to an intervention, such as a participant's motivation to change. Of course, the very process of placing subjects into a treatment or control condition requires that there be sufficient numbers of potential participants to have a statistically meaningful outcome. Small sample sizes, even with randomization, do not allow for effective comparisons. Given a large enough sample size, random assignment allows researchers to assume that the treatment and control groups are comparable and that differences observed in the groups after an intervention can be attributed to the impact of the program.

Given the advantages of RCTs, they continue to be upheld as the strongest form of research evidence in favor of a program (O'Connell et al., 2009). However, RCTs have drawbacks as well. They are time and resource intensive, and there can be significant logistical challenges with randomization. For example, in school settings it may not be possible to randomly assign individual students to receive an intervention because students are already grouped into classrooms. Furthermore, in some cases RCTS may not be feasible, and they may not be able to answer important questions pertaining to the reasons why particular outcomes were obtained (e.g., why did urban families respond positively to a parenting program but rural families did not?). Additionally, many applied—as compared with research—programs fail to have a sufficient number of participants in each condition (treatment, control) to be able to have sufficient statistical analysis power to conduct a proper analysis.

Other Research Designs. Given the drawbacks and challenges of designing and implementing RCTs, other research designs are commonly employed in evaluating prevention programs. For example, in a pre–post design, an outcome measure (i.e., posttest) is compared with the same measure taken at the beginning of the study (i.e., pretest). In Chapter 2, we describe other types of research designs that are commonly employed in evaluations of prevention programs. In addition to these more basic designs, a plethora of more sophisticated statistical procedures have become increasingly popular. For example, advances in growth curve modeling allow researchers to more accurately track development over long time periods. With growth curve modeling, it is possible to follow research participants over the course of time—even a lifetime—through varied developmental stages to draw implications for prevention.

Clinical Expertise

Applying clinical expertise is a second component that contributes to evidence-based practice. As defined by the IOM (2001), clinical expertise is "the ability to use clinical skills and past experience to rapidly identify each patient's unique health state and diagnosis, individual risks and benefits of potential interventions, and personal values and expectations" (p. 147). The APA Task Force on Evidence-Based Practice (2006) describes clinical expertise in terms of the ability to link best research evidence to patients' individual circumstances and preferences. That is, clinical expertise

> is essential for identifying and integrating the best research evidence with clinical data (e.g., information about the patient obtained over the course of treatment) in the context of the patient's characteristics and preferences to deliver services that have the highest probability of achieving the goals of therapy. (p. 275)

Clinical expertise is developed through a variety of experiences, including scientific and clinical training, knowledge and understanding of theory, knowledge and understanding of current research, clinical experience, and self-reflection (APA, 2005).

Clinical expertise for psychologists has been described in terms of the multiple competencies that contribute to positive outcomes (APA, 2005). These competencies include the following:

- Assessment, diagnosis, and treatment planning
- Treatment implementation and monitoring
- Interpersonal skills
- Self-reflection and improvement
- Application of current research evidence
- Understanding the influence of cultural, contextual, and individual differences on treatment
- Seeking additional resources as needed
- A cogent rationale for treatment decisions

We expand briefly on each of these competencies with an emphasis on how they may be applied in a prevention context.

Assessment, Diagnosis, and Treatment Planning

One aspect of clinical expertise involves appropriate assessment, diagnosis, and treatment planning given the individual circumstances and needs of the participants. In a prevention context, this may involve an evaluation of the risk and protective factors for the targeted population to determine the most pressing needs and to gauge the level(s) of prevention efforts (e.g., universal, selective, indicated) that is necessary. Given this information, an appropriate prevention plan may be developed, including screening participants, selecting an evidence-based prevention program, and developing a plan for evaluating the outcomes of the program.

Consider a school counselor who wants to implement a bullying prevention program at school. (Note that we would recommend that counselors work with an implementation team to select, develop, and implement a comprehensive bullying prevention program; however, for the purposes of this example, we refer to a single counselor.) A sensible first step in developing a plan would be to survey students, teachers, parents, and school staff to gauge the extent of bullying occurring at school. Questions may assess what kinds of bullying are happening, when and where it is happening, and how serious the incidents are. The counselor should evaluate risk and protective factors, such as current school policies against bullying and how connected students and adults feel to the school. Once these data are collected, the counselor may decide to pursue a multilevel prevention approach, including a universal program for all students and a selective program to work individually with students who have been involved in bullying incidents in the past. The counselor may use different approaches across levels of prevention. For example, for the universal level of prevention, the counselor may use a research-supported manualized program. For the selective level of prevention, a more eclectic approach may be employed that is built around evidence-based practices but does not rely on a treatment manual.

Treatment Implementation and Monitoring

Once a prevention plan has been selected or developed, it should be implemented with skill and flexibility, and incremental outcomes should be evaluated. In the case of the bullying prevention plan, the counselor should collect data in formal and informal ways throughout the course of the implementation. This may include conversations with students and teachers, reviews of discipline incidents, and intermittent follow-up surveys. If aspects of the plan do not appear to be working, appropriate adjustments should be made. For example, if student engagement in the universal program appears to be low, the counselor may decide to interview students to determine what aspects of the program are not resonating with them. A skilled mental health worker will make on-the-fly adjustments to match the needs and preferences of participants while remaining in harmony with the objective and process of the program.

Interpersonal Skills

Interpersonal skills are a key component of clinical expertise. The ability to form a therapeutic alliance, to facilitate effective communication, and to foster a positive sense of the future are essential proficiencies for psychologists, counselors, social workers, and other mental health workers. A mental health worker who excels in these competencies is likely to boost the effectiveness of prevention programs, while an unskilled facilitator can undermine the benefits of programs that have otherwise been shown to be clinically effective. For example, a counselor who cannot maintain a positive rapport with students who have engaged in bullying will likely not be able to run an effective group session aimed at preventing the recurrence of this behavior. Examples of clinical skills for prevention leaders to demonstrate include the ability to do the following:

- Build relationships; for example, demonstrate empathy, emphasize positive motivation and expectations, match leaders' language to the language of the group.
- Gather information about the groups and participants; for example, understand motivation and purposes for maintaining status quo or making changes.
- Maintain structure; for example, provide rationales, break large tasks into small steps, maintain focus, engage all participants.
- Teach new skills; for example, describe goals and activities in clear and understandable language, model the behaviors, provide rationales, check for comprehension.
- Ensure implementation; for example, personalize the discussions, anticipate problems and prepare participants for how to manage change challenges, modify the program to fit the needs of the participants.

Self-Reflection and Improvement

The practices of self-reflection and improvement contribute to the development of clinical expertise. Psychologists, counselors, social workers, and other mental health workers should actively reflect on their practices, thoughts, beliefs, and emotional reactions. Furthermore, this self-reflection should lead to seeking out new skills that may improve one's practices. In the school counselor example, self-reflection may lead the counselor to realize that he or she does not have enough knowledge or training to specifically deal with antigay bullying in schools. Self-reflection should lead to seeking out resources to improve on one's practice.

Application of Current Research Evidence

Skilled mental health researchers also seek out current research evidence to support their prevention practice. Prevention workers should be adequately trained in research methods to consider and evaluate clinical evidence of a practice or program's effectiveness. Building off of the above example, the school counselor who seeks out information about preventing antigay bullying may investigate the literature on this topic and identify the approach that has the most compelling research support. This individual exhibits clinical expertise by integrating this knowledge into one's current context.

Understanding the Influence of Cultural, Contextual, and Individual Differences on Treatment

Understanding the influence of patient and contextual characteristics, including cultural and individual differences, is another aspect of clinical expertise. There is no one-size-fits-all approach to advancing mental health. Programs and practices that have been demonstrated as effective in some contexts may not generalize to other circumstances. Clinical expertise contributes to the ability of the counselor or psychologist to foresee potential problems and adapt programs as needed. If a bullying prevention program has only been shown to be effective in a very different cultural setting, the counselor must be prepared to evaluate how these cultural differences may affect the outcomes of a local implementation. Cultural, contextual, and individual differences may significantly affect the likelihood of success of a given program. A skilled mental health worker takes these factors into consideration in a selection and implementation of new practices and programs.

Seeking Additional Resources as Needed

Knowing when to ask for help is a feature of clinical expertise. Like the example of the counselor who realized that she did not have sufficient knowledge to address antigay bullying in her school, mental health workers should pursue additional resources as needed to increase the likelihood that a prevention program will be successful. Resources may come in the form of additional knowledge or may extend to seeking clinical supervision of attempts at new approaches, employing consultants, making a referral, or engaging in professional development training. While costly, professionals should avail themselves of national conferences, conventions, and professional development workshops to learn about the wide array of prevention programs and services available. The cutting-edge work of developing programs is often presented at conventions long before it is available in published form.

A Cogent Rationale for Treatment Decisions

Finally, clinical expertise encompasses a cogent rationale for treatment decisions. As described in the above competencies, prevention activities should be well reasoned and not left up to chance. Although midcourse corrections may be necessary, treatment decisions should follow a rational plan that is guided by theory, research, and one's professional experience and expertise.

Patient Characteristics, Values, and Preferences

Accounting for patient characteristics, values, and preferences is the third facet of evidence-based practice. According to the APA (2005), these characteristics include a patient's "specific problems, strengths, personality, sociocultural context, and preferences" (p. 2).

When selecting and implementing a new prevention program, psychologists, counselors, and other mental health workers are faced with several questions on how to take these into consideration. These questions may include the following:

- To what extent may individual characteristics play a role in influencing the outcome of this program?
- How similar is the population I am working with to the population utilized for research evaluations? To what extent may these cultural differences play a role in influencing the outcome of this program?
- To what extent does this program take into account developmental considerations that are relevant to the population I am targeting (e.g., age appropriateness)? (APA Presidential Task Force on Evidence-Based Practice, 2006)

While it may not be possible to decisively answer all of these questions for a given program, taking the time to think through them undoubtedly contributes to the development of a prevention plan that is more responsive to the needs and preferences of the targeted population. In the next sections, we briefly discuss the role of individual characteristics, population characteristics, and developmental considerations on selecting and implementing evidence-based prevention programs.

The Role of Individual Characteristics

Individual characteristics may moderate the impact of a preventive intervention. These characteristics include race, ethnicity, culture, gender, gender identity, sexual orientation, family context, and religious beliefs, along with many other possible influences. In implementing a universal prevention program with a diverse audience, it may not be possible to tailor the program to each participant's individual preferences. At the same time, if programs are not relevant to participants, it is unlikely that they will be successful. Furthermore, as prevention programs become more intensive (i.e., selective and targeted interventions), they should necessarily become more attuned to the unique needs and characteristics of the participants. For example, consider a targeted prevention program designed to help students who are at high risk for dropping out of school. This type of intervention should take into account the unique circumstances of each individual: What barriers are hindering the student? What skills need to be practiced? What resources can be called on? Is this a problem of boredom, financial crisis, family conflict, depression, or other factors? By considering the individual characteristics of each participant, a comprehensive prevention plan can be developed and implemented.

As an example, consider a student who has social interaction difficulties. What individual characteristics play a role in these difficulties? One factor could be a skills deficit. Has the student not had the opportunity to learn the necessary skills to engage in appropriate social interactions? Or does the student have the skills but becomes so anxious and tense that he is unable to use the skills when they are needed? Or a third possibility may be that the student knows the skills and could use them but elects to not use the skills as a means of exerting power or influence over a situation. The observed absence of a skill may be a result of any of these three or even more explanations, and the prevention activities to address the lack of evident skills must be modified depending on the reason for the absence.

In much of therapy, interventionists may experience what they call "resistance to change" and attribute the problem to be the client. In prevention work, we generally take a different perspective on the concept of resistance. If there is insufficient engagement, the problem isn't considered a resistant client but a failure of the facilitator or program to meet the needs of the target audience. We may not have selected an appropriate intervention, we may have moved too quickly in presenting change requests, or the change process may be threatening because it does not fit the expectations of participants. In short, responsibility for delivering an effective prevention program rests with the prevention provider and requires attention to the needs of the individuals, the group, or the community. The change process is selected with all of these characteristics in mind. If the program is not appearing to be effective, it is the responsibility of the change leader—the preventionist—to adjust the program or select another process.

The Role of Population Characteristics

Just as individual characteristics may influence the outcomes of a given program, population characteristics also may influence how successful a program is. In selecting a prevention program, the program facilitator should evaluate the degree of similarity between the tested and the targeted population. If the program has demonstrated impact with a population that is dissimilar to the intended population, the generalizability of the research findings may be limited. Nationality, race/ethnicity, location (e.g., country, region; rural, suburban, urban), and other population factors affect the relevance of prevention program components. For example, a parenting program that works for rural families in the U.S. South may not work for families in inner-city settings, and a parenting program developed with a middle-class Caucasian group may not be deemed appropriate for an African American community, and vice versa. A community intervention that works in Ireland may not work in Ghana; similarly, a program in one neighborhood may be very inappropriate with another neighborhood just down the street. Prevention program facilitators should ensure that the program they are interested in implementing aligns with the context of the cultural values and traditions of the population to be served. Making cultural adaptations, also known as translation, may be needed to make a program more appropriate to a new population. This process is discussed in Chapter 4.

The Role of Developmental Considerations

Evidence-based prevention programs should take into account developmental considerations, and prevention workers should evaluate the appropriateness of the program, given the development and life stage of the targeted population. The timing of prevention efforts is important. Consider a program that is designed to prevent substance use and abuse by children and adolescents. It may be too late to begin preventive efforts in high school, when many adolescents may have already experimented with drugs and alcohol. Many programs aim to prevent problems before they begin (e.g., efforts to increase exercise in healthy young people), while other programs target populations that exhibit warning signs (e.g., exercise programs for people with prediabetes). Prevention workers should select programs that match the developmental and risk profile of the targeted population. The intellectual, cognitive, and social development of participants should also be taken into consideration when choosing a prevention program. Program materials should be appropriate for the intended population. The language used to talk to adolescents about fostering healthy relationships may not be the same as the language used to talk to older adults. As with other individual and population characteristics, the process of translation may be necessary to ensure that a prevention program is relevant to and meets the developmental needs of participants.

Summary

This chapter has described three components of evidence-based prevention based on definitions from IOM and APA. Evidence-based prevention involves the application of best research evidence, given clinical expertise and consideration of patient characteristics, values, and preferences. It is critical that this level of information be available in descriptions of evidence-based programs so that potential users have the opportunity of selecting programs most appropriate to their needs.

Activity

Consider the three components common to IOM's and APA's definitions of evidence-based programs: (1) scientific research, (2) clinical expertise, and (3) patient characteristics, values, and preferences.

- How would you rate the importance of each of these components? Do you favor some components over others, or do you weigh them all equally? Why?
- How do you evaluate your ability to access and interpret best research evidence?
- How do you evaluate your own level of clinical expertise?
- How do you evaluate your ability to assess the characteristics, values, and preferences of individuals and populations that you work with?

2
Evaluating Qualitative and Quantitative Research Methods

Mark Twain popularized the quote, "There are three kinds of lies: lies, damn lies, and statistics" (1906/2006). This level of skepticism is not warranted with regard to the vast majority of prevention research, but it does point out that just because something is stated as a research finding, that does not make it fact. In this chapter, we provide an overview of some of the information that consumers of research evidence should consider when evaluating the quality of a research study. First, we describe types of data that may be gathered in a research study, including qualitative and quantitative data. Next, we consider the quality of the prevention evidence, including threats to the internal and external validity of a study, and we describe common study designs. The goal of this chapter is to provide a broad overview of some of the most common considerations that impact the quality and trustworthiness of prevention research. It is beyond the scope of this chapter to provide a comprehensive description of all aspects of research quality and study design. However, we hope that readers are able to use the information contained in this chapter to become more informed consumers of journal articles, news reports, and other descriptions of research findings. Furthermore, we hope that this overview will assist readers in considering issues of quality as you design and engage in your own prevention research.

Kinds of Prevention Evidence

There are two major forms of data that are typically employed in prevention research, qualitative data and quantitative data. Both can be used to help answer some of the most important questions related to the prevention of mental health problems, such as the following:

- How common are these problems?
- How do these problems develop?

- What prevention programs work? Which ones prevent problems from ever occurring? Which ones work to lessen the negative consequences of preexisting problems?
- Who do these programs work for?
- Under what conditions do these programs work?

Research methods associated with qualitative and quantitative data have developed out of distinct methodological traditions, and researchers engaged in these traditions may have different philosophies regarding the nature of knowledge, the purpose of research, and other core beliefs. However, both types of evidence may be used to contribute to the knowledge base pertaining to prevention in the mental health field.

Qualitative Evidence

Qualitative evidence may be derived from people reporting their experience and thoughts about an issue (Patton, 2002). The data are typically in the form of language. Examples of qualitative evidence include interviews, focus group discussions, and open-ended questionnaires. Qualitative studies are typically seen as an exploratory form of research; they tend to be used to generate rather than test hypotheses (Patton, 2002).

Qualitative research has several advantages. Qualitative methodology recognizes the importance of the perspectives of the research participants along with the researchers. Qualitative research offers participants choice over what they want to share, in what ways, and at what depth (Ponterotto, 2005). In this way, it may be seen as respectful and responsive to participants' experiences. Qualitative research also tends to be more flexible, allowing for midcourse corrections as needed. For example, the researcher may make changes to the research plan if participants indicate that there are additional facets of the studied phenomenon that are not adequately being probed. This type of flexibility is less common in quantitative studies.

As is true with any form of data, use of appropriate procedures for analysis is essential for deriving meaningful conclusions from qualitative data. There are a number of procedures for analysis of qualitative data, including those informed by grounded theory, critical theory, and ethnography (Ponterotto, 2005). A commonality among these procedures is the careful review of research participants' comments on the topic being addressed and the search for themes emerging from these comments. The emerging themes are thought to be indicative of meaningful aspects of participants' experiences.

Example of a Qualitative Study Related to Prevention

A simple form of qualitative research was used to assess the impact of a tertiary preventive intervention with hospitalized patients who were suffering from persistent severe mental illnesses, including schizophrenia and bipolar disorder (Waldo & Harman, 1999). The intervention focused on preventing the patients' symptoms from causing poor relationships with other patients and the hospital staff. This was a tertiary prevention effort because it was not focused on preventing or curing the patients' illnesses but, instead, was focused on limiting the negative effects those illnesses had on their relationships. Patients and staff were trained in communication skills that have been shown to improve relationships in other settings (Guerney, 1977). Several weeks after the training was completed, the researchers interviewed staff members and asked what, if any, changes they perceived among the patients. Through qualitative analysis, themes were identified in the staff's responses about the patients, including that the patients seemed more forthcoming with their concerns, were more understanding of each other, and were more cooperative with staff (Waldo & Harman, 1999).

Quantitative Evidence

Quantitative evidence is evidence that can be counted. Examples of quantitative data include the number of people suffering from a mental illness, how often people experience psychological symptoms, or how participants rate the usefulness of a preventive intervention on a scale of 1 to 5. A great advantage of quantitative data is that it can be easily summarized. For example, means and standard deviations can be used to describe the number of minutes of exercise that a group of participants engage in. This summary information is simple to calculate, easy to understand, and is seen as being objective. A second advantage of quantitative data is that different groups can be compared in a straightforward manner. For example, consider a large corporation that wants to offer a program promoting an active lifestyle to its employees in the hopes of reducing health care costs and days of work missed due to illness. The corporation can easily distribute surveys to employees asking about their current level of activity to determine which locations are in most need of the program. In this way, resources can be distributed to the areas that need them most. Furthermore, the same survey can be readministered at a later time to compare the level of activity before and after the implementation of the program. This evidence can be used to help draw conclusions regarding how well the program works.

Using Qualitative and Quantitative Evidence

Qualitative and quantitative evidence can be used in complementary ways to evaluate preventive interventions. Often quantitative data are used to determine if a preventive intervention was successful, and qualitative data are used to help understand why or why not. In the active lifestyle program example described above, qualitative data may be used to help describe the quantitative findings. If the program resulted in positive changes for some participants but not others, qualitative data may be collected to help explain this result. Perhaps, the program worked better in certain regions of the country because the suggested healthy activities—say, taking a daily walk around the neighborhood—are better suited for some settings (e.g., areas with a mild climate, safe streets, etc.) than for others. Qualitative data may provide contextual information that was not captured via quantitative methods.

Example of a Prevention Study Using Qualitative and Quantitative Evidence

A preventive intervention for people entering helping professions focused on teaching mindfulness practices in a small group setting (Newsome, Waldo, & Gruszka, 2012). It was hoped that learning mindfulness practices would increase participants' self-acceptance as they faced the stresses associated with trying to help others. The effectiveness of the intervention was assessed by using a quantitative measure of participants' levels of self-compassion prior to and after the training. The results indicated that participants showed a statistically significant increase in their self-compassion in response to the mindfulness training. The research included a qualitative component in that participants were asked to describe their experience of receiving the training. Qualitative analysis of the participants' comments helped explain how the mindfulness training affected the participants' self-compassion. They indicated that the group helped them become aware of when they were "putting themselves down," and taught them the value of self-care (Newsome et al., 2012).

A combination of qualitative and quantitative evidence may also inform the development of prevention efforts. A common form of prevention research combining these forms of evidence is *needs assessment* (Romano & Hage, 2000). Needs assessment provides epidemiological evidence regarding what needs a particular group of people have and how well those needs are being met. Often needs assessments employ a *triangulation model* (Goodman, Wandersman, Chinman, & Imm, 1996). The triangulation model is based on the premise that the needs of a group of people can best be understood, or "fixed," by observing them from three vantage points. Those vantage points are (1) existing records and/or publications about the groups' needs, (2) the opinions of "key informants" (people who have contact with and are knowledgeable about the group), and (3) members of the group themselves. Typically, both qualitative and quantitative data about needs are gathered. The qualitative data may be gathered through interviews with members of the group who might be helped through a preventive intervention and with key informants. Quantitative data in the form of questionnaires can also be gathered from both these groups. Qualitative and quantitative data can also be gathered from records that are routinely kept on the people in the group, and/or previous studies that have been published about them.

Consider a prevention worker who wants to conduct a needs assessment regarding the prevention of adolescent drug use. Using the triangulation model, the preventionist might gather the evidence from the following sources:

- Peer-reviewed journal articles and scholarly books
- Local and national police records regarding drug-related arrests of adolescents
- Interviews with adolescents, parents, and teachers
- Surveys of adolescents, parents, and teachers

It is desirable that the needs assessment include the perspectives of those who have been affected by the problem (i.e., adolescents who have abused drugs) as well as those who are the intended audience of the intervention (i.e., children who would participate in an antidrug program). Relating back to the components of evidence-based prevention described in Chapter 1, needs assessment can help prevention workers connect best research evidence to the needs and preferences of the group targeted for intervention.

Quality of Prevention Evidence

Evaluating evidence regarding prevention from prior research requires understanding the strengths and limitations of that research. When examining the quality of research evidence, two major questions can be asked (Cook & Campbell, 1979). First, "Are the findings of the research study true?" This question is related to internal validity. Internal validity refers to our confidence in making causal statements based on the results of the study (Heppner, Kivlighan, & Wampold, 2008). In other words, the concept of internal validity is related to how likely it is that the results of a study were really due to the intervention, as opposed to other explanations. Studies that are able to unambiguously demonstrate how one variable causes changes on another are considered to have high levels of internal validity. For example, consider a study that showed that a relationship skills program for incoming college students was related to the participants reporting (a) fewer conflicts with their roommates, (b) fewer psychological problems, and (c) better grades than a control group that did not receive the intervention. If we believe that this study had a high level of internal validity, we will be more likely to conclude that the relationship skills training, rather than other factors, directly contributed to the positive outcomes.

The second question is "Are the findings of the research useful?" This question is related to external validity. External validity refers to the generalizability of the results of a study (Heppner et al., 2008). That is, to what degree do we think that we could obtain similar results if we were to repeat the study with different people in a different setting? For our relationship skills example, if we believe that the study had a high level of external validity, we would expect that the same relationship skills training would produce similar outcomes on other college campuses. It is also desirable for a program to work under "real-world" circumstances (e.g., implemented by the resident advisors who supervise the dorms at each college) rather than only in more controlled environments (e.g., implemented by the developer of the program).

It is important to note that evidence of internal and external validity falls along a continuum. Aspects of research design may contribute to or detract from internal and external validity, and there can be a trade-off between enhancing one form of validity at the expense of the other. In the following sections, we describe threats to the internal and external validity of prevention research and ways of reducing those threats. Understanding these threats and how they can be mitigated allows people to make a more informed judgment regarding how much faith to place in research findings. This critical evaluation of the quality of research evidence is essential to conducting evidence-based prevention.

Threats to Internal Validity

The internal validity of a study is threatened to the extent that plausible alternatives exist to explain the results of the study. For example, given the results of the relationship skills training, what other factors could have caused the positive results that were observed? Threats to the internal validity of research studies have been extensively described by a number of authors (Cook & Campbell, 1979; Gelso & Fretz, 1992; Heppner et al., 2008). The most common threats are described below and related to prevention research. Given each type of threat, we describe how these factors may affect the interpretation of the results of the relationship skills training study.

History. History refers to outside events, unrelated to the intervention, which cause changes in participants during the course of the research study. In the relationship skills training example, other external factors may influence the quality of the relationships among college freshman independent of any impact of the intervention. Major national crises, like the terrorist attacks on 9/11/2001, have been shown to be related to people pulling together, appreciating each other, and supporting each other (Park, Aldwin, Fenster, & Snyder, 2008). If such an event occurred during the training, improvement in the students' relationships could have been the result of a reaction to those events rather than the training. Smaller and more local events may also represent a threat to internal validity, such as a change in university policy, making it easier for students living in the dorms to change roommates.

Maturation. Maturation refers to naturally occurring changes in people related to the passage of time instead of the impact of the intervention. Using the relationship skills example, it is possible, even likely, that college students' relationships improve as they become more familiar with each other and learn new ways of relating. This natural growth occurs independent of any training they might receive. Maturation is a threat to internal validity in that researchers could mistakenly believe that changes occurring from natural maturation are the result of their preventive intervention.

Mortality. Mortality, also known as attrition (Heppner et al., 2008), occurs when participants who differ in important ways drop out of research study at different rates. The danger is that the participants for whom the program is not working are more likely to drop out than the participants who are gaining from the program. When dissatisfied participants drop out before the end of the program and the posttest, this makes the program look more beneficial than it was in reality. In the example of the relationship skills training, mortality would be a threat if the students with the most troublesome relationships dropped out of the study at a higher rate than students with healthier relationships. The dropouts, had they remained, would be likely to have the lowest posttest scores of the group. If this is true, their withdrawal from the study would result in higher overall posttest scores for the remaining participants, independent of any improvements to the relationship skills of the remaining participants.

Testing. In some cases, the act of participating in an assessment may produce changes in the respondents. When people take a test, there is the possibility that it could affect the way they think and act regarding the area that was tested. In the case of relationship skills training, it is possible that the act of taking the preassessment might cause participants in the program to start focusing more on those relationships and trying to improve them. If this is the case, changes in their posttest scores could possibly be influenced by the act of taking the pretest, independent of the effects of the actual training.

Instrumentation. Lack of accuracy of assessment procedures can also be a threat to the internal validity of prevention research. Tests that are not adequately reliable can generate different scores over time, regardless of any actual change to what is being measured. This can be a problem with both qualitative and quantitative methods, and qualitative research may be particularly vulnerable. Because assessment is made by the researcher through interpretation of qualitative data, it is possible that changes in the researcher's perspective could affect assessment. For example, a researcher who is aware that students have received relationship skills training may be inclined to see positive effect of that training in the qualitative data that the students provide about their relationship experiences, even if there has been no change in the students' relationships.

Selection. Some threats to internal validity are related to the way that participants are selected for control and treatment groups. Some preventive interventions are offered to people who are interested in them rather than through random assignment. These motivated participants may then be compared with a "control" group composed of people who were not interested in participating in the program. The problem is that these groups may differ in important ways. It is possible that the effects of the program were brought about by preexisting differences in motivation rather than the actual training. In the case of the relationship skills training, it would not be ideal to compare motivated college students who chose to participate in the intervention with unmotivated participants who opted out. If the treatment group reported higher levels of relationship satisfaction than the control group at the end of the study, it would be unclear if the intervention caused improvements, or if the types of people who participated in the program were simply more responsible and conscientious than the types who did not want to participate.

Selection is a critical threat to the internal validity of prevention studies because it can interact with other threats. For example, people who are interested in participating in an intervention may have developmental differences (i.e., maturation) or have different reactions to outside events (i.e., history) than people who are not interested in the intervention. To lessen the impact of selection problems, it is critical that treatment and comparison groups be essentially equivalent. Randomly assigning participants to treatment and control groups is the best way to mitigate problems with selection (Heppner et al., 2008). When people are randomly assigned to groups, it is believed that any preexisting characteristics that might affect the outcome of the study will also be evenly distributed across the treatment and control groups. Therefore, these external influences should affect the treatment and control groups in approximately the same ways, making it less likely that they will bias the results of the study in favor of one group over the other.

Threats to External Validity

The external validity of prevention studies is determined by how well the findings of the studies generalize to situations in the real world. Three major aspects of generalizability are population, setting, and time (Cook & Campbell, 1979). That is, can the results of the study be generalized to other groups of people? In different settings? At different times? We consider each of these aspects and associated threats to external validity in turn.

Threats Associated With the Selection of Participants. One aspect of external validity relates to the population of participants included in the study. If a large number of participants representing a diverse population were included in the evaluation of the program, we may feel more confident that similar results may be obtained if we implement the intervention elsewhere. On the other hand, if the group of participants was small and homogeneous, we may be less certain that other participants will respond in the same way. Ideally, the participants in a research study will adequately represent the diversity of the population that the intervention is intended for. To the extent that the participants do not represent the intended audience of the intervention, the external validity of the study is compromised. In the case of the relationship skills training, we may feel confident that results of a study conducted at a large state university will likely generalize to another large state university. We would be more skeptical that the results would translate to a completely different targeted population—say, men who have been arrested for domestic violence. While the college students who are developing new relationships might show improvements in response to the training, the relationships of men who have been arrested for domestic violence may be more troubled and less likely to change in response to the same training.

Threats Associated With Differences in Setting. A second aspect of external validity relates to the setting in which the implementation takes place. Interventions may have a different impact based on where and how they are conducted. The more similar the conditions of implementation are to real-world settings where the intervention might take place, the more confident we are that the results will generalize. Considering our relationship skills training example, it is likely that results of a study in which implementation of the program takes place on a college campus facilitated by counseling center staff would generalize to a similar implementation at a comparable university. However, the results of this study might not do a very good job of informing what results may be expected if the program were to be implemented in a prison setting with men arrested for domestic violence. The difference in these two settings—college residence hall versus prison—is vast. Counselors, psychologists, and social workers considering adopting a prevention programs should consider the representativeness of the study setting to their own circumstances.

Threats Associated With Differences in Time. A final aspect of external validity relates to the time in which the study implementation takes place. We previously described how important outside events, such as the September 11 terrorist attacks, may cause changes in study participants unrelated to the impact of the study. These types of events can also interact with how people respond to an intervention. A program may have more or less resonance depending on the cultural factors that are at play when it is implemented. For instance, the relationship skills training program may be received differently on campus during a time when young people are feeling unified as opposed to when there is a substantial societal turmoil. It is also worth noting that as times change, the impact of interventions may change as well; it is likely that a relationship skills training program that was developed in the 1960s would need to be updated in order to remain relevant to an audience of college students today.

Study Designs

Threats to internal and external validity are influenced by the design of the study. Understanding the validity threats associated with different study designs allows prevention workers to become informed consumers of research. Two key questions are (1) How much can I trust these findings? (2) How much confidence do I have that these findings are relevant to my circumstances? In considering these questions and how they relate to study designs, it is important to note that there may be some inherent conflict between maximizing internal and external validity. One way to increase internal validity is to tightly control the conditions of the study, which helps rule out other possible explanations for the results. However, these tightly controlled conditions may not closely resemble the real-world circumstances in which the program may be applied, thus decreasing external validity. Researchers can enhance the external validity of studies by conducting them under realistic conditions in practice settings, but it may then be difficult to control all the variables that could offer alternative explanations for the findings. In short, multiple studies are often needed to provide different sorts of evidence related to internal and external validity—some conducted in controlled setting emphasizing internal validity and some conducted in practice settings emphasizing external validity (Gelso & Fretz, 1992).

In this section, we summarize some common types of research designs that may be encountered in evaluations of prevention programs. Our goal is to assist readers in their ability to critically evaluate research findings in light of the two key questions mentioned above. For each study design described below, the trade-offs between enhanced internal and external validity are identified.

True Experimental Designs

RCTs involve random assignment of participants to treatment and control groups, and they typically include a pretest and one or more posttest measures. RCTs are considered to be "the gold standard" when it comes to evaluating treatments because they are thought to protect against many of the threats to internal validity (Norcross, Beutler, & Levant, 2006). When threats to internal validity are minimized, we can more confidently make strong causal statements linking the impact of the intervention to the observed results.

Two of the features of RCTs that contribute to internal validity are the use of comparison groups and random assignment. These features help rule out history, maturation, and some other threats to internal validity. Under random assignment, it is assumed that there are no important measured or unmeasured differences between the groups prior to the preventive intervention. A pretest can establish whether there are differences in the measured constructs prior to intervention. Given a large enough sample size, we assume that any unmeasured differences in participants that would be relevant to the study would be distributed evenly across the treatment and control groups via randomization.

Positive results from RCTs are widely considered to be some of the strongest forms of evidence in support of a preventive intervention. We will see this in Chapter 3 when we discuss the Society for Prevention Research standards for efficacy, effectiveness, and dissemination, and in Chapter 4, when we discuss the selection criteria used by registries of evidence-based programs. However, it is important to note that RCTs do not protect against all threats to internal and external validity. For example, one of the criticisms of RCTs in clinical psychology is that the participants in RCTs are not adequately representative of patients seeking treatment in practice. Westen (2006) argues that stringent exclusion criteria of RCTs disqualifies many typical patients from participating in RCTs. The implication is that these studies may lack a high degree of external validity with regard to the intended audience of the treatment. In other words, the study population is too different from the targeted population to be able to generalize the results of the evaluation.

Quasi-Experimental Designs

The time-series design and nonequivalent control group design are two commonly used quasi-experimental designs (Cook & Campbell, 1979). Quasi-experimental designs are very similar to experimental designs, but they lack the random assignment of participants to treatment models that is true of experimental designs.

Time-Series Design. In the time-series design, multiple observations are collected over time. A basic type of time-series design involves a single treatment group and no control group. A series of assessments takes place before the intervention begins. These pretests form a baseline that represents the initial status of each individual. After the intervention is completed, another assessment is collected to determine the immediate impact of the program. Additional assessments occur at regular intervals to track how long any changes last after the end of the program.

When a preventive intervention is being evaluated using a time-series design, ideally participants will show little change during the period prior to the start of the preventive intervention and will show dramatic positive change after the intervention. For example, children involved in an effective preventive intervention intended to raise self-esteem would show little change in their self-esteem prior to the intervention and a rise in self-esteem directly after they participate in the intervention. Time-series designs offer protection against some threats to internal validity. Using the example of the children and the self-esteem program, if the children's self-esteem was rising naturally as they got older (maturation), they likely would have shown improvement at the baseline before the intervention. If assessing children's self-esteem caused it to rise (testing), again it would have changed prior to initiation of the preventive intervention.

A time-series design was used to assess the impact of a mindfulness group on the self-compassion of people training to enter helping professions (Newsome et al., 2012). Repeated measures of participants' self-compassion showed no changes during the 4 weeks before they received mindfulness training. After the mindfulness training, significant improvements in self-compassion were observed. Because the participants' self-compassion did not change during the period prior to the involvement in the mindfulness group, it is reasonable to assume that independent of intervention, their levels of self-compassion were relatively stable. The fact that participants' levels of self-compassion rose dramatically after they participated in the mindfulness group offers evidence that the mindfulness group was responsible for raising their self-compassion.

Time-series designs can be of particular value in circumstances where randomization is not possible. For example, if we are interested in finding out the impact of strict driving under the influence (DUI) laws on rates of drunk driving, it is not possible to randomly assign certain states to different laws. Instead, we may identify a state that has recently enacted a new law and compare rates of drunk driving before and after it went into effect. While this design can help us make inferences in situations where randomization is not possible, it has some weaknesses with regard to internal validity. Time-series designs cannot control for all external influences that may influence the study findings. For example, in the case of the new DUI law, the timing of the law may have coincided with a sharp economic downturn, which may also influence rates of drunk driving.

Nonequivalent Control Group Design. In the nonequivalent control group design, a treatment group is compared with a control group, but random assignment is not employed. Both groups are assessed before and after the intervention. Ideally, the groups will be similar on the pretest measure. It may be necessary to statistically control for any systematic differences between groups on the pretest (or if groups are radically different, meaningful comparison may not be possible). If the groups are reasonably comparable on the pretest, and the treatment group is significantly improved in comparison to the control group on the posttest, this finding suggests that the intervention had a positive effect.

This design was used to assess the impact of a secondary prevention intervention for men who had been arrested for domestic violence (Waldo, 1988). A judge offered men who were arrested for domestic violence an opportunity to participate in a relationship skills group to avoid having a permanent record of their offense (the experimental group). These men were compared with men whose legal status was handled by another judge who did not offer them the opportunity to participate in the group (the control group). Men's involvement in domestic violence prior to the preventive intervention (pretest) was assessed from their legal records. All the men from both the experimental and control groups had engaged in domestic violence. Men's involvement in domestic violence after the preventive intervention was also assessed (posttest) from their legal records. During the year following the preventive intervention, 20% of the men who did not participate in the relationship skills group had a subsequent arrest for domestic violence. None of the men who participated in the group had a subsequent arrest.

Similar to the time-series design, the nonequivalent control group design may be useful in cases where random assignment is not possible. Connecting back to the study regarding the impact of a new DUI law, it may be fruitful to compare rates of drunk driving in the state that is implementing the new law with a comparable state that has not changed its laws. This comparison may reduce some of the threats to internal validity. For example, if rates of drunk driving are unchanged in a state that is experiencing a similar economic downturn, we may have more confidence that this historical event is not substantially impacting rates of drunk driving in the state with the new law.

Despite its advantages in some situations, the nonequivalent control group design does have limitations. Because random assignment is not employed, there may be important differences between the treatment and control groups. These differences may be observable or unobservable. In short, there can be a large number of competing explanations for the results of a study that are unrelated to the impact of the intervention.

Preexperimental Research Designs

Preexperimental designs are titled "preexperimental" because they have so many threats to internal validity that it is questionable if they can be employed to determine cause-and-effect relationships. Nevertheless, preexperimental studies may provide some types of information regarding preventive interventions. Although preexperimental studies are far from "the gold standard," they are often conducted due to their relative simplicity to implement. In this section, we describe three types of preexperimental studies: (1) the one-shot case study, (2) the one-group pretest posttest, and (3) the static group comparison.

One-Shot Case Study. The one-shot case study is a preexperimental design that involves assessing people who have experienced an event in an effort to assess the impact of the event. The qualitative study of relationship skills training with hospital patients and staff described earlier in the book is an example of a one-shot case study (Waldo & Harman, 1999). The hospital staff was asked to assess the patients' relationship skills after the patients and staff had received relationship skills training. The advantage of this design is that it is simple, quick, and takes very little preparation. For these reasons, it fits in well in clinical settings and can be used to evaluate most interventions. The disadvantage is that it does not control for most threats to internal and external validity, including history, maturation, and selection. For example, the hospital patients in the social skills training example may have been developing improved social skills as they become accustomed to living within the hospital (maturation), not because they participated in social skills training.

Because they cannot prevent threats to the internal validity, one-shot case studies are typically not accepted as strong evidence that a preventive intervention works. They may, however, help identify which interventions deserve further study and which do not. If assessment after an intervention suggests that participants are very low on the quality that the intervention was intended to promote, this could suggest that the intervention needs to be modified or even abandoned. For example, if hospital staff reported that after relationship skills training, patients were more argumentative with each other and less cooperative with staff, this information could be taken into account when considering continuing the program.

One-Group Pretest Posttest. The one-group pretest posttest is another commonly used preexperimental design. The one-group pretest–posttest design improves on the one-shot case study by providing pretest assessment for comparison with the posttest assessment. Participants in a preventive intervention are measured before they participate and again afterward. If they show significant improvement, this is seen as evidence that the intervention was effective. However, like the one-shot case study, the findings of studies that use this type of design should be interpreted with caution, as this design fails to minimize many of the threats to internal validity.

A secondary prevention study of military personnel who had engaged in domestic violence used the pretest–posttest design (Waldo, 1986b). Participants' perpetration of domestic violence was assessed before and after they received group training in anger management, expressive speaking, and empathic listening skills. Their involvement in domestic violence reduced significantly after participating in the group, suggesting that the participants learned skills in the group that helped them avoid being violent again. These results are promising, but there are other explanations that cannot be ruled out. For example, it is possible that the military command began stressing that domestic violence was unacceptable among service members during the time this study was being conducted (history), or the process of being identified as having engaged in domestic violence, rather than the content of the intervention (maturation), may have motivated the participants to change. Still, the reduction in domestic violence after the group training suggests that the intervention is worthy of additional study. On the other hand, if the number of domestic violence incidents that the participants perpetrated had increased after they were in the group, it would suggest that the group should be modified or discontinued.

Static Group Comparison. A third preexperimental research design, static group comparison, involves assessing one group that has had a particular experience and comparing their scores to another group that has not had that experience. For example, a researcher may investigate whether people who witnessed domestic violence as children are more likely to also report engaging in domestic violence as an adult than those who did not. The static group comparison design is also often referred to as a correlational design, because it assesses the correlation (or association) between two variables. It is worthwhile here to repeat the popular adage, "correlation does not imply causation." The use of the term *correlation* or *association* is appropriate with regard to this design because this language conveys that the design cannot assess whether one variable *causes* another, only that one variable *is associated with* another. Despite this limitation, this kind of design can be very useful, especially in epidemiology. For example, the correlational domestic violence study can offer potentially important information for targeted prevention efforts. If men who witnessed violence tend to be more violent, then preventive interventions can be offered to these men, perhaps focusing on providing them with healthy, nonviolent models of family interaction.

The static group comparison of men who witnessed violence and those who did not witness violence does not prove that witnessing violence causes people to become violent later in life. There are too many threats to the internal validity of this design that preclude strong statements about causation. Despite its limitations, the static group comparison is valuable because it allows for investigation of naturally occurring events that researchers cannot and/or would not want to cause. A classic example is the association between smoking and negative health effects. Since the early days when smoking research suggested smoking has negative health effects, researchers have not been willing to assign some people to smoke. However, many people do choose to smoke, and comparing their health status to nonsmokers has provided compelling data on the effects of smoking. The static group comparison allows researchers to collect information on unhealthy or undesirable events like smoking or domestic violence without causing them. That information can then be used to design prevention programs which, in turn, can be evaluated using more rigorous study designs.

The Conflict Between Internal and External Validity and the "Bubble Hypothesis"

As discussed earlier, in terms of study design researchers may face trade-offs between internal and external validity. Researchers want to be able to make strong causal statements relating an intervention to positive outcomes while ruling out competing explanations. Efforts to maximize internal validity may involve imposing restrictive conditions on the implementation of the study—for example, by excluding from the study individuals who have characteristics that might interact with the intervention (i.e., have more than one diagnosed mental health problem). However, to the extent that the excluded individuals represent a typical patient, the external validity of the study may be compromised. When interventions are conducted in field settings under realistic circumstances, it is much harder to control for external influences and rule out competing explanations of the study results.

This tension between internal and external validity in research has been likened to an air bubble under a parking sticker on a car windshield (the "bubble hypothesis"; Gelso & Fretz, 1992). Pushing on an air bubble under a parking sticker typically does not get rid of it but moves it to another spot under the sticker. Similarly, efforts to minimize threats to internal validity may amplify threats to external validity and vice versa. One answer to this dilemma is to conduct multiple studies to build a record of positive evidence, with some studies focused on especially promoting internal validity and some focused especially on promoting external validity.

Take, for example, prevention researchers who believe that helping men who have engaged in domestic violence learn relationship skills would prevent future violence. Ideally, the researchers would like to conduct an RCT in a domestic violence treatment facility to provide strong evidence about how well the program works. However, treatment facilities may be reluctant to engage in a resource-intensive intervention (involving, e.g., assessing men's relationship skills, randomly assigning participants to treatment and control groups, and implementing the program) in the absence of prior evidence that the training works. To build a positive record in favor of their program, the researchers could first study whether relationship skills are associated with positive interpersonal relations in another setting, like university residence halls, where students are likely to be more available to engage in assessment (Waldo & Fuhriman, 1981). If relationship skills are associated with better relations, then the researchers could use a quasi-experimental design to test if students who choose to receive relationship skills training develop better relationship than a nonequivalent control group (Waldo & Morrill, 1983). If the relationship skills training works with students in the residence halls, then the researchers could go on to use a preexperimental pretest–posttest design to assess if relationship skills training is associated with improved skills, enhanced relationships, and reductions in violence among men who have engaged in domestic violence (Waldo, 1988).

In this example, the researchers have more control when conducting studies in the residence halls, so they can promote internal validity. But the residence halls studies may not have external validity in that their findings cannot be confidently generalized to treatment of men who have engaged in domestic violence. The preexperimental study conducted with men who have engaged in domestic violence has a higher degree of external validity because it was conducted in a treatment setting with the actual men, but there are threats to the study's internal validity (e.g., history, maturation, etc.) because of the design. However, taken together, these studies offer more compelling evidence for the effectiveness of the relationship skills training. The training in more controlled setting provided evidence of internal validity, and the training in the practice provided evidence of external validity.

_____ **Conclusion**

This chapter has focused on describing some of the considerations that contribute to the trustworthiness and applicability of research findings. Prevention research may involve qualitative and/or quantitative data, and the research design will have implications for the internal and external validity of the study. A convincing record of evidence regarding the positive effects of a prevention program may be amassed over the course of several studies. Ideally, the studies will involve research designs that allow for strong causal statements to be made and will address different aspects of internal and external validity. In the next chapter, we will describe some common features of effective prevention programs and discuss the Society for Prevention Research standards for efficacy, effectiveness, and dissemination. These standards directly relate to the issues of quality that have been described in this chapter. For example, there is a strong emphasis on employing experimental and quasi-experimental study designs. Furthermore, the standards take into account the potential for tension between internal and external validity by distinguishing between studies that have demonstrated efficacy (i.e., positive results under tightly controlled conditions) and effectiveness (i.e., positive results under more naturalistic conditions).

Activity

Select several journal articles that describe evaluations of preventive interventions in an area that interests you. After reading through the articles, answer the following questions for each of the studies:

- What types of data were collected?
- What was the study design?
- How would you respond to the question, "Are the findings of this research study true?" In what ways are threats to internal validity minimized? What other explanations for the research findings are plausible?
- How would you respond to the question, "Are the findings of this research study useful?" In what ways are the results of the study able to be generalized? What threats to external validity might be problematic?
- If you were the researcher, how would you design your next study to bolster the evidence of the positive impact of the program?

3

Criteria for Evidence-Based Practice and Programs

In the previous chapter, we presented a general overview of some of the considerations that impact the quality of prevention research. In this chapter, we present two different but complementary conceptualizations of what makes a prevention program effective. First, we describe nine characteristics identified by Nation et al. (2003) as being common to effective prevention programs. Next, we describe the set of criteria for program efficacy, effectiveness, and dissemination developed by the Society for Prevention Research (Flay et al., 2005). Finally, we present a classification matrix that can be used to organize research evidence.

Common Features of Effective Prevention Programs

Nation et al. (2003) conducted a review of reviews to identify common features of effective prevention programs. The scope of the research was limited to universal and selective programs aimed at preventing specific problems in adolescents (i.e., substance abuse, risky sexual behavior, school failure/dropout, and delinquency/violence); however, the features identified in the review appear to have broad applicability to prevention programs in general. They identified nine principles organized into three broad categories:

- Principles related to program characteristics
  - Comprehensive
  - Varied teaching methods
  - Sufficient dosage
  - Theory driven
  - Focused on enhancing positive relationships
- Principles related to matching the program with the targeted population
  - Appropriately timed
  - Socioculturally relevant

- Principles related to implementation and evaluation of prevention programs
  - Outcome evaluation
  - Well-trained staff

In the next sections, we briefly elaborate on each of these principles.

Principles Related to Program Characteristics

Effective prevention programs are comprehensive, utilize varied teaching methods, involve sufficient dosage, are theory driven, and are focused on enhancing positive relationships.

Prevention programs should be sufficiently comprehensive to be impactful. The ecological model (Bronfenbrenner, 1979) posits that multiple levels of influence, such as individual, family, peer, and community characteristics, play a role in the development of mental health issues. Therefore, to prevent these problems, programs should target multiple levels. For example, an obesity prevention program will be more likely to be successful if it takes into account family and community factors as well as individuals' beliefs and behaviors. All people know how to lose weight to become healthier: They do so by eating fewer calories and exercising more. Yet even with that knowledge, we still have obesity. A program to address the issue has to focus on the characteristics of the individual, what she or he believes about a healthy body ("I was born this way" or "I have heavy bones"), the family ethos ("clean your plate . . . think of the starving children"), and the community characteristics ("feed a family of four for $10 at a fast-food restaurant").

Effective prevention programs employ varied teaching methods. In particular, Nation et al. (2003) indicated that successful programs tend to include active role playing where participants practice specific skills related to the prevention goal, such as communication skills for resisting drug use. We know that passive learning is less powerful than engaged experiences and that modeling, role-playing, and increased similarity to actual experiences create increased change potential.

Prevention programs are more likely to be successful when they involve sufficient dosage. Dosage refers to the number of contact hours of the program and includes aspects such as the number of sessions, the length of sessions, and the total duration of the program. Many successful programs include an initial intensive training period, followed by periodic "booster" sessions. For example, one of our projects included a "booster session" 3 months after completing a family group program as a way of bringing family members back to remind them of the skills they had mastered and provide them with encouragement to continue to previously effective skill implementation they had mastered.

Effective prevention programs should be driven by theory. A sound theoretical rationale should drive the types of activities that are included in the program and how these activities are expected to contribute to the preventive process. Adopters of programs should ask the questions: Why should this program work? Is it grounded in theory in such a way that the outcomes are predictable given the issues being addressed?

A common thread of the effective prevention programs reviewed by Nation et al. (2003) is that they focus on fostering positive relationships. This component may be particularly relevant for programs aimed at young people. However, in all prevention activities, encouraging strong, positive relationships is an important goal. As we strive to help people achieve their potential, we should remember that healthy relationships serve as powerful protective agents against mental health problems. One of the most thoroughly researched programs in healthy living and obesity reduction is the Pritikin Plan (http://www.pritikin.com/home-the-basics/about-pritikin/how-pritikin-works.html). While the plan addresses diet and exercise, it also emphasizes relationships and personal stress management as core aspects of achieving and maintaining healthy lifestyles. In fact, the model places as much emphasis on the social/personal characteristics for maintenance as it does on the physical/dietary components.

Principles Related to Matching the Program With the Targeted Population

Effective prevention programs are appropriately timed and socioculturally relevant. In the previous chapter, we discussed the importance of cultural and developmental concerns in prevention efforts. That is, prevention programs should include activities that are culturally sensitive and developmentally appropriate, given the targeted population. This, of course, requires connectedness and familiarity with the community and people one will be working with as the program is conceived, developed, and implemented. To provide engagement, we encourage cofacilitation with a community member if one of the leaders is not from the community or not connected with the participants. This is an example of demonstrating respect and regard for the community and provides the opportunity for cross-training by engaging local facilitators to work within the community.

Principles Related to Implementation and Evaluation of Prevention Programs

Effective prevention programs involve well-trained staff and incorporate outcome evaluation. The quality of the staff that is implementing a program can have a profound impact on the program's outcome. A prevention program should include facilitators who are selected on the basis of their ability to connect to participants and implement the program skillfully. Furthermore, extensive training and supervision can help ensure that facilitators implement the program with fidelity and are prepared for the sometimes unpredictable nature of prevention work. Furthermore, process and outcome evaluation data can assist program administrators in monitoring the implementation of the program and making corrections as needed. Outcome data—both positive and negative—contribute to the body of evidence supporting the prevention program. Positive results support the use of the program; negative results may indicate that the program is ineffective or that it requires modification for use with the targeted population. For additional information on features of effective prevention programs, readers are referred to Book 7 in this Toolkit, *Program Development and Evaluation in Prevention* (Conyne, 2012).

Society for Prevention Research Standards of Evidence for Efficacy, Effectiveness, and Dissemination

In the previous section, we described a set of descriptive principles associated with effective prevention programs based on a review of programs for preventing emotional and behavioral problems in adolescents. In this section, we summarize a more proscriptive set of standards for identifying prevention programs as efficacious, effective, and ready for dissemination developed by the Society for Prevention Research. The Society for Prevention Research is an international organization made up of researchers, practitioners, and policy makers, among others. The mission of the organization is to advance understanding of the etiology and prevention of problems in various health-related fields, including mental health, physical health, social well-being, and academic achievement. Furthermore, the group promotes the translation of this information to advance health and well-being. More information about the organization may be found at http://www.preventionresearch.org/.

In 2005, the Society for Prevention Research published a set of standards for identifying evidence-based programs (Flay et al., 2005). These standards, which are listed in Table 3.1, are divided into three levels:

1. Standards for identifying programs as being efficacious (21 required standards, 30 total)

2. Standards for identifying programs as being effective (31 required standards, 43 total)

3. Standards for identifying programs as being ready for dissemination (34 required standards, 47 total)

These levels are organized as a hierarchy. The first level is efficacy. To meet the criteria for being "tested and efficacious," a program must meet 21 required standards. The criteria related to efficacy are especially concerned with enhancing internal validity. That is, the program is first evaluated on the strength of the causal statements linking the intervention with

Table 3.1 Society for Prevention Research Standards of Evidence for Efficacy (EY), Effectiveness (EV), and Dissemination (DI)

Standards	EY	EV	DI
Specificity of the efficacy statement			
Statement of efficacy is of the form "Program X is efficacious for producing Y outcomes for Z population"	X	X	X
To claim effectiveness, studies must meet all conditions of efficacy trials plus additional criteria		X	X
To claim readiness for dissemination, studies must meet all criteria for effectiveness plus additional criteria			X
Program description and measures			
Program described at a level that would allow others to implement/ replicate it	X	X	X
Manuals, appropriate training, and technical support readily available		X	X
Intervention delivered under conditions expected in the real world		X	X
Theory of causal mechanisms is stated		X	X
Statement of "for whom?" and "under what conditions?" the intervention is effective		X	X
Evidence of ability to go to scale			X
The stated public health/behavioral outcome(s) of the intervention is measured	X	X	X
Includes at least one long-term follow-up measure	X	X	X
Psychometrically sound measures	X	X	X
Valid measures of the targeted behavior	X	X	X
Adequate reliability: Internal consistency (alpha), test–retest reliability, and/or interrater reliability	X	X	X
At least one form of data collected by people independent of the intervention	X	X	X
Level of exposure measured in both treatment and control conditions		X	X
Integrity and level of implementation/delivery of the intervention	x	X	X
Engagement of the target audience and subgroups of interest is measured	x	X	X
Measures of mediating variables (or immediate program effects) are included	x	x	x
Measures of potential side-effects are included	x	x	x

Standards	EY	EV	DI
Multiple measures of constructs are included	x	x	x
Measures of moderating variables are included		x	x
Clarity of causal inference			
Research design allows for unambiguous causal statements	X	X	X
At least one comparison condition does not receive the tested intervention	X	X	X
Assignment to conditions maximizes confidence in causal statements. For most interventions, random assignment is necessary. For some kinds of research, repeated time-series designs without randomization, regression discontinuity designs, or matched control designs with pretest equivalence may be acceptable	X	X	X
Generalizability of findings			
Report specifies what/who the sample is and how it was obtained	X	X	X
Real-world target population and the method for sampling it is explained		X	X
Degree to which findings are generalizable is evaluated		X	X
Reports of subgroup analyses are included	x	x	x
Experimental dosage studies/analyses are conducted		x	x
Replication with different populations		x	x
Replication with different program providers		x	x
Precision of outcomes			
Main effects analysis at the same level as the randomization and includes all cases	X	X	X
Tests of pretest differences and adjustments for them if necessary	X	X	X
When appropriate, adjustments are made for multiple comparisons	X	X	X
Analyses minimize the possibility that effects are due to attrition	X	X	X
Extent and patterns of missing data are reported	x	x	x
Statistically significant effects			
Results are reported for every measured outcome	X	X	X
A consistent pattern of statistically significant positive effects is observed	X	X	X
No serious negative (iatrogenic) effects on important outcomes are observed	X	X	X

(Continued)

Table 3.1 (Continued)

Standards	EY	EV	DI
Demonstrated practical public health impact	X	X	X
Some evidence of practical importance is demonstrated		X	X
Clear cost information is readily available	*x*	*x*	X
Costs and cost-effectiveness analyses are reported		*x*	X
Significant effects for at least one long-term follow-up	X	X	X
At least two high-quality studies meet all of the criteria for efficacy	X	X	X
The preponderance of evidence is consistent with the results of the two highest quality studies	X	X	X
Consistent findings are reported from at least two different high-quality effectiveness trials		X	X
The more replications the better	*x*	*x*	*x*
Independent replications are conducted by organizations adopting programs			*x*
Monitoring and evaluation tools are available to providers			X
The factors expected to ensure program sustainability are reported			*x*

Source. Adapted from Flay et al. (2005, pp. 170–171). Copyright 2005 Society for Prevention Research. Prevention science by Society for Prevention Research. Reproduced with permission of Plenum Publishers (journals) in the format Journal via Copyright Clearance Center.

Note. Required standards are designated with upper case Xs. Desirable standards are designated with lower case italicized *x*s.

the results. Efficacious programs have demonstrated with a reasonable degree of certainty that the effects of the intervention have caused positive outcomes.

The next step in the hierarchy is effectiveness. To meet the criteria for being "tested and effective," a program must meet all the efficacy standards plus additional standards related to effectiveness, for a total of 31 required standards. Once a program meets the efficacy criteria, it is next evaluated under more naturalistic conditions. Effective programs have demonstrated with a reasonable degree of certainty that the effects of the intervention have caused positive outcomes under realistic circumstances.

The final step in the hierarchy is readiness for dissemination. To meet the criteria for being "tested, effective, and ready for dissemination," a program must meet all of the effectiveness standards plus additional standards related to dissemination, for a total of 34 required standards. The criteria related to readiness for dissemination are especially concerned with the adequacy of resources to support widespread distribution of the intervention.

Programs that are ready for dissemination have demonstrated with a reasonable degree of certainty that the effects of the intervention have caused positive outcomes under realistic circumstances and that there are adequate resources to support broader adoption of the program.

In the next sections, we briefly summarize the types of evidence required at each of the three levels in the hierarchy. We refer interested readers to the full description of the standards for additional information (Flay et al., 2005).

Criteria for Efficacy

The Society for Prevention Research proposes 21 required standards and 9 desirable standards for a program to meet the criteria for efficacy. As discussed in Chapter 1, *efficacy* refers to the positive outcomes of a program under ideal circumstances. The goal of a successful efficacy trial is to be able to state with a reasonable degree of confidence which positive outcomes may be ascribed to the impact of the program and not other irrelevant causes. In a broad sense, the efficacy standards relate to designing studies in a manner that minimizes the potential impact of external influences and clarifies the connection between the intervention and its outcomes.

The standards are divided into five domains: (1) specificity of the efficacy statement, (2) program description and measures, (3) clarity of causal inference, (4) generalizability of findings, and (5) precision of outcome. In this section, we briefly elaborate on some of the criteria under each domain.

Specificity of the Efficacy Statement. An efficacious program should have a clearly defined efficacy statement that specifies what outcomes the intervention has effected for which populations. The efficacy statement should only describe outcomes that have actually been measured. For example, a middle school dropout prevention program cannot be said to actually prevent dropout unless follow-up data have been collected to show a reduction in dropout, rather than intermediary results (e.g., increases in school connectedness). It may be tempting for researchers to imply additional impact than what was measured; this standard helps to establish clear connections between what was tested and what outcomes were obtained without embellishment.

Program Description and Measures. An efficacious intervention should be clearly described and involve psychometrically sound measurement and data collection. Important components of this area include (a) a description of the program that is detailed enough to allow others to replicate it, (b) the collection of long-term follow-up data, and (c) the use of measures that display adequate reliability and validity evidence. In examining how much detail to provide in written descriptions of a program that is being made available for implementation, we recommend that the directions and activities be clear enough so that a person reading the material could, without consultation, conduct the program in reasonably the same fashion as the program developer had done when originally developing and implementing the program.

Clarity of Causal Inference. An efficacious intervention should be designed in a manner that allows strong causal inferences to be developed. This area is concerned with the appropriate design of the study and how threats to the validity of results are mitigated. The design must involve a control group, and the preferred research design involves random assignment to control and intervention groups. In cases where random assignment is not possible, a limited number of alternate designs are acceptable (i.e., repeated time-series design, regression discontinuity, matched control design), given adequate attention to threats to validity.

Generalizability of Findings. An efficacious intervention should clearly identify the sample, including subgroups (e.g., age, sex, race/ethnicity, socioeconomic status [SES], and any other relevant risk characteristics). A clear description of the sample helps readers evaluate the extent to which the outcomes of the study may generalize to their own circumstances. This standard requires that the evaluator seek the demographic information along with other relevant participant characteristics prior to operation of the project.

Precision of Outcome. An efficacious program should produce outcomes that may be unambiguously attributed to the impact of the intervention. Important components in this area include (a) appropriate statistical procedures, (b) statistically significant results, (c) practically significant results, (d) results that extend beyond the end of the intervention period, and (e) replication of positive results over at least two different studies. There can be a rush to publish positive findings without taking the time to replicate the project. This standard establishes the replication requirement to help ensure that positive results represent a true finding rather than a chance occurrence.

Summary. For a program to qualify as being "tested and efficacious" according to the Society of Prevention Research standards, it must demonstrate its quality and impact across several domains. The program must be very clearly described from start to finish, including the sample, study design, data collection methods, psychometric properties of the measures, data analysis plan, and outcomes. Within each of these areas, the program must meet stringent criteria. Furthermore, long-term results must be demonstrated, and more than one study must produce positive results.

Criteria for Effectiveness

The Society for Prevention Research proposes 31 required standards and 12 desirable standards in order for a program to meet the criteria for effectiveness. These requirements are listed in Table 3.1. This set of standards includes all of the required criteria for efficacy, plus additional criteria related to effectiveness. *Effectiveness* refers to the positive outcomes of a program under real-world circumstances. The goal of a successful effectiveness trial is to be able to state with a reasonable degree of confidence which positive outcomes may be expected as a result of the program for a given population under realistic circumstances. Broadly, the effectiveness standards are concerned with designing studies that shed light on "for whom" and "under what circumstances" a given program works. We briefly touch below on some aspects of the criteria for effectiveness.

Program Description and Measures. An effective program is useful to practitioners under real-world circumstances. To that end, intervention manuals should be detailed enough for practitioners to be able to implement the program. Descriptive materials should clearly describe for whom the program is intended and under what conditions it has been shown to work. Furthermore, it may be appropriate to offer training and technical assistance to support practitioners implementing the intervention in applied settings.

Effectiveness trials should also measure participants' level of exposure to program activities, including how closely the implementation followed the intervention manuals and how involved participants were with regard to the intervention activities (e.g., did everyone participate in group discussion, take-home activities, etc.). Because the program is being implemented in real-world settings, it is important to document variations in implementation that may influence results. We have found that program developers, as a consequence of lengthy involvement in the development process, establish skills and methods that may not be fully described in the implementation manual. The following is an example of this problem from an experience in developing a family program for families with disruptive children. After the training materials were developed and ready for dissemination, a graduate student made an important observation. In the parenting groups, the program developer always took the time to connect with every family member in the group, including a brief session summary that included each family member in a review of what had occurred during the session and how recommendations may be carried out during the following week. The developer was so consistent in this exercise that some team members referred to the activity as a closing ritual, yet in the dissemination materials, there was no mention of this as a specific technique to include in the implementation program. These small procedures can have a major impact on program implementation.

Generalizability of Findings. Effectiveness trials should provide practitioners with information regarding the impact of the program for different populations. In large effectiveness trials with a heterogeneous sample of participants, researchers may investigate whether the effects of the program differ by subgroup. Replications of effectiveness trials using different targeted populations may also be informative. Furthermore, researchers may study how different modes of delivery (i.e., classroom setting vs. virtual setting, nurses vs. social workers as facilitators) affect outcomes. In all of these cases, processes and outcome should be clearly documented to assist practitioners in determining how well the program may work, given their particular set of

circumstances. It is equally important for researchers to monitor characteristics of the intervention that might fluctuate and result in differential outcomes. In one of the family studies, we had very positive outcomes with two
family group programs, but a third application resulted in very disappoint-
ing outcomes. When examining differences, it became clear that the clinical
skill level of the third group of intervention specialists was less refined and
less connected to the treatment population than for the facilitators of the
earlier two implementation teams. This difference led the program developers to change the recommendations related to minimal skills for program
interventionists to make the requirements more stringent.

Precision of Outcome. An effective program should demonstrate positive
results over at least two effectiveness trials, and the reported results should
be limited to only those variables actually measured.

Summary. For a program to qualify as being "tested and effective" by the
Society of Prevention Research, it must demonstrate its value in real-world
settings. It must meet the requirements for an efficacious program, as well
as additional criteria. It should be clearly described in enough detail for a
practitioner to implement the program and to evaluate its potential usefulness for a particular population and context. Furthermore, it must produce
positive results over more than one effectiveness study.

Criteria for Dissemination

The Society for Prevention Research outlines 34 required standards and
13 desirable standards for a program to meet the criteria for being ready for
broad dissemination. These standards are listed in Table 3.1. Programs that
are *ready for broad dissemination* have been shown to be efficacious and
effective and have the resources and support materials to suggest that the
widespread distribution of the program is feasible. The criteria at this level
include all of the standards for efficacy and effectiveness, plus several additional standards, which are briefly described below.

Program Description and Measures. A program that is recommended for
widespread dissemination has demonstrated evidence of readiness to go to
scale. This criterion of "readiness to go to scale" includes widespread availability of manuals and the ability of practitioners and organizations to
receive training and technical assistance related to successfully implementing
the program. This is often a difficult criterion to meet because researchers
who conduct efficacy and evaluation studies very seldom have the capacity
or infrastructure to also support dissemination or implementation efforts.
Rather, programs that have been demonstrated to be impactful are typically
made available through commercial distributors. These distributors may be
more focused on the marketing of the materials than on the collaborative or

consultation aspects of the process, unless they include consultation/training components as part of their public offering.

Precision of Outcome. For a program to be widely disseminated, practitioners should have access to detailed information related to the costs of the program. Costs may include training, materials, staff time, and other direct and indirect expenses. Practitioners may use this information to weigh the costs with the potential benefits and compare the program with other interventions.

Furthermore, to encourage continued monitoring of the outcomes of the intervention, program developers should make monitoring and evaluation tools available to practitioners. As practitioners monitor and report their own findings, the research base on the impact of the program will continue to grow.

Summary. For a program to qualify as being "tested, effective, and ready for dissemination" by the Society of Prevention Research, it must demonstrate both its value and its feasibility to be applied broadly. Support and resources in many forms, such as manuals, training and technical assistance, detailed cost information, and monitoring and evaluation tools, must be available to justify the costs of dissemination and to help increase the likelihood that implementations of the program will be successful.

A Classification Scheme for Organizing Research Evidence

In the above section, we discussed two sets of principles for effective prevention. In addition to meeting standards of evidence, it is also important that the prevention programs selected for implementation are appropriate according to theory. Prevention is a rich area of study, and prevention research focuses on a wide variety of topics and processes. While this richness is part of the attraction of studying prevention, it also can be overwhelming, resulting at a minimum in failure to recognize important relationships between research findings and at worst in debilitating confusion that discourages further inquiry. Organizing prevention research in a conceptual framework can help researchers and practitioners manage and interrelate research findings. The concepts of *context* and *function* can be used to form a classification scheme for organizing prevention research.

Research Context

Prevention activities may take place within and across multiple contexts, including biological, psychological, and sociocultural (National Institute of Mental Health, 1998). Risk and protective factors—factors that contribute to the development of mental health problems or make them less likely—exist at each of these levels. Examples of biological risk and protective factors include genetic predispositions, substance and alcohol abuse, nutrition, exercise, environmental toxins, and psychopharmacology. Examples of psychological risk and protective factors include traumatic experiences, neglect, locus of control, self-esteem, and self-efficacy. Sociocultural risk and protective factors include family dysfunction, poverty, prejudice, religion, social networks, and community resources. Furthermore, within each of these contexts, multicultural and individual variables such as developmental level, gender, ethnicity, and SES play a vital role. Prevention programs should address the multiple contexts in which risk and protective factors occur (Kellam & Van Horn, 1997), or they should indicate clearly where they have been examined and where they have not so that practitioners developing plans to implement a program are clear in where the program may—and may not—actually work.

Research Function

Prevention research can also be categorized according to the function being studied: preintervention epidemiology, preventive intervention, and prevention service delivery system (National Institute of Mental Health, 1998). *Preintervention epidemiology research* examines the prevalence of a problem and/or risk and protective factors related to the problem and the relationships between risk and protective factors. *Preventive intervention research* examines prevention interventions at the universal, selective, and targeted levels. *Prevention services delivery system research* examines the organization, effectiveness, and efficiency of systems for delivering prevention services.

Preintervention epidemiology research lays the groundwork for future prevention efforts and is especially important in emerging areas of research. For example, a relatively new topic in the literature on bullying is cyberbullying. If a school counselor wanted to prevent cyberbullying, a first step might be examining the limited research on multiple risk and protective factors found in the literature. Mishna, Khoury-Kassabri, Gadalla, and Daciuk (2012) found that students involved in cyberbullying were, for example, more likely than other peers to use the computer for more than 2 hours a day and to give their password to a friend. This study provides information that, combined with additional research, can lead to informed interventions.

Preventive intervention research examines what works and for whom. For example, someone may define a secondary/indicated prevention program for those at high risk for bullying that is highly effective. If someone uses that program in a different context (i.e., a different region of the country and/or in another cultural context), it may not be successful. There are some prevention topics where a large number of intervention programs exist and some conclusions can be taken from the preponderance of research. For example, Ttofi and Farrington (2011) conducted a meta-analysis of bullying prevention programs. They concluded that there are some best practice components of bullying prevention interventions that lead to success. For example, school antibullying policies, high dose and intensity of teacher training, classroom management, improved playground supervision, and parent involvement and training. One of the benefits of this meta-analysis is that it provides information regarding what prevention interventions (e.g., primary/universal focused on classroom management) and what service delivery components were successful (e.g., teachers). Future research on prevention interventions could ask the question what interventions work within specific contexts.

The Classification Matrix

The levels (biological, psychological, and sociocultural) and functions (preintervention, preventive intervention, and prevention services) described above can be used to form a matrix for categorizing prevention research, as developed by Waldo and Schwartz (2003) and presented in Table 3.2. The levels and functions categorized in the matrix can guide researchers toward literature they need to examine prior to conducting studies and help them identify future directions for research based on their findings. Each category of research is informed by and informs the others. For example, knowledge of epidemiology guides preventive intervention innovation and evaluation. Then, when viable interventions have been identified, research can turn to examination of service delivery systems. In turn, the efficiency and effectiveness of prevention service delivery systems can be assessed by examining their impact on epidemiology. The interactive process between the categories offers a logical progression for prevention science and can guide systematic prevention research (National Institute of Mental Health, 1998). Two critical questions that can help determine the value of studies on epidemiology, preventive interventions, and service delivery are What is the public health significance of the study? And, to what extent does the study maximize scientific opportunity?

The prevention matrix can be used by practitioners to evaluate their prevention goals and find evidence-based prevention programs that match their objectives. It can also be used to identify holes in collective knowledge about prevention. For example, we may have research evidence demonstrating that preventive interventions can increase self-esteem, but we may not know how increases in self-esteem relate to improved physical health or social adjustment, or what is the most effective and efficient preventive service delivery system for increasing self-esteem. Last, the matrix can be used to guide research in the systematic acquisition of prevention knowledge. For example, epidemiological research can identify which variables should be the target for preventive interventions. Intervention research can determine which universal, selective, and targeted prevention interventions are most efficacious for impacting those target variables. Service research can assess the effectiveness and efficiency of different approaches to delivering the efficacious interventions. Epidemiological research can assess the impact that intervention service delivery systems have on the prevalence and strength of risk and protective factors in specific populations.

Table 3.2   Prevention Research Matrix

Context (e.g., Gender, Race, Ethnicity, SES, Sexual Orientation)	Function		
	Preintervention (Epidemiology, Understanding Relationships Between Variables and Causes)	Preventive Intervention (Primary-Universal, Secondary-Selective/Indicated, Tertiary-Indicated)	Service Delivery Systems (Dissemination, Implementation, Effectiveness, Health Economics)
Biological development: risk and protective factors (e.g., genetics, physiology, nutrition, exercise, psychopharm)			
Psychological development: risk and protective factors (e.g., personality, locus of control, attitude, motivation)			
Sociocultural development: risk and protective factors (e.g., family, affiliations, school, work, community)			

Source: Adapted from "Best practice guidelines on prevention practice, research, training, and social advocacy for psychologists," by S. M Hage, J. L. Romano, R. Conyne, M. Kenny, C. Matthews, J. P. Scwartz, and M. Waldo, 2007, *The Counseling Psychologist, 35,* p. 493–566. Copyright 2007 Division of Counseling Psychology. Reproduced with permission.

While the matrix can guide programs of systematic prevention research, it is not possible or necessary for all prevention researchers to systematically address all the contexts and functions depicted in the matrix in their studies. It is important, however, that prevention research be informed by previous studies addressing contexts and functions, that current studies' contributions to illuminating contexts and functions are clear, and that the holes in understanding contexts and functions that can be addressed through subsequent research be identified. In this way, the matrix can provide a guide allowing different research teams in different locations at different times to contribute to systematic understanding of prevention.

The Classification Matrix in Practice: Examples From Prevention Research

Both theory (Sullivan, 1938) and research (Guerney, 1977) have suggested that the ability to communicate effectively improves interpersonal relations and could help prevent problems in a wide variety of areas in people's lives. To test this assumption, we have conducted and are conducting research on prevention through improving communication in interpersonal relations. Our research corresponds with the categories offered by the prevention research matrix as follows:

Epidemiology

To begin with, epidemiological research was conducted to assess the association between the quality of people's interpersonal communication and their health (biological development), emotional adjustment (psychological development), and relationships (social development). Preliminary research showed that college students who reported more positive relationships with their roommates had significantly less emotional difficulties and significantly better communication when confronting each other about difficult issues (Waldo & Furhiman, 1981). Subsequent research found a significant relationship between the quality of communication between college roommates and problems with alcohol (biological development), depression (psychological development), and perceptions of the residence halls social environment (social development; Waldo, 1984). Additional research demonstrated a relationship between the quality of communication between roommates and academic achievement (grade point average) and retention at the university (Waldo, 1986a). Taken together, these findings suggest that preventive interventions designed to improve communication and enhance relationships between roommates could prevent biological problems with alcohol abuse, psychological problems like depression and poor school performance, and social problems like poor roommate relationships and negative feelings about residence halls.

Preventive Interventions

Based on the epidemiological findings described above, a series of studies was conducted on the preventive effects of Relationship Enhancement (Guerney, 1977) communication skills training. Primary, secondary, and tertiary preventive interventions have been studied. Examples of each are described below.

Primary Prevention. Primary prevention studies were conducted that focused on the use of the Relationship Enhancement communication skills training to improve communication between college roommates. These were primary prevention studies because there was no reason to believe that the students had already had significant roommate problems or were especially prone to have problems in the future. Instead, the intervention was designed to prevent problems with communication in roommate relationships before they happened.

(Continued)

(Continued)

First a pilot study with 14 students was conducted and demonstrated that Relationship Enhancement communication skills training could be conducted in residence halls (Waldo & Morrill, 1983). Next, a quasi-experimental study was conducted with 215 students (Waldo, 1985). The study compared experimental and nonequivalent control groups of students' communication prior to and following Relationship Enhancement communication skills training. This was a quasi-experimental design because the students were not randomly assigned to the experimental and control conditions. The experimental group reported improved communication in comparison with the control group. A follow-up primary prevention study was conducted (Waldo, 1989). A total of 98 students were randomly assigned to receive Relationship Enhancement communication skills training, and 120 students were randomly assigned to a wait list for training later. The study employed a pretest–posttest design. The study found significant improvement in the experimental groups' communication in comparison with the wait list control group before the wait list control group received training. The study also found that when members of the wait list control group later received Relationship Enhancement communication skills training, their communication improved as well. This study suggested that the training improves communication between roommates. Given the previously identified association between roommates' communication and their biological (less problems with alcohol), psychological (less problems with depression), and social (less roommate problems and negative feelings about the residence halls) well-being, there is reason to believe that this preventive intervention could have pervasive beneficial preventive effects for students.

Secondary Prevention. Given the success of Relationship Enhancement communication skills training as a primary prevention intervention, we employed it for secondary prevention. Secondary prevention focuses on preventing an existing problem from continuing and getting worse. Our focus has been on use of Relationship Enhancement communication skills training to prevent problems with domestic violence from continuing and getting worse. Researchers and the agencies in which they conduct research are often unwilling to randomly assign their clients to a no treatment control condition. This is especially true with domestic violence, where injury and possible death are the consequences of failure to prevent reoccurrence of the problem (Waldo, 1987). For this reason, we employed preexperimental and quasi-experimental designs to evaluate secondary prevention interventions with men who have engaged in domestic violence. One study used a preexperimental pretest–posttest design to assess the impact of Relationship Enhancement communication training with military personnel who had engaged in domestic violence (Waldo, 1986b). Results indicated that the men achieved significant improvements in their communication skills (psychological development) and their communication with their partners (social development) following training. More important, they showed significant decreases in the number of abusive incidents they engaged in directly following training, and the decrease was maintained through a 3-month follow-up period. Because abusive incidents occurred with their partners and resulted in bodily harm, this change can be seen as improvements in both social and biological development. A second study employed a quasi-experimental nonequivalent control group design (Waldo, 1988). In this study, 90 men who had been arrested for one incident of domestic violence were compared. Because of differences in the way judges handled their cases, 60 of the men were referred for Relationship Enhancement communication skills training and 30 were not referred. Out of the 60 who were referred, 30 followed through on receiving training, and 30 never sought the training. The domestic violence rearrest rates during the year following the training were assessed for all the men. Results indicated that the men who went through the Relationship Enhancement communication training had significantly fewer rearrests for domestic violence (0%) than did the men who were not referred for training (20%) or the men who were referred for training but never participated (20%). Again, because domestic violence is a social event with biological consequences, reduction in domestic violence incidents can be considered an improvement in biological and social development. Despite the fact that these studies are not true experiments, taken together they do offer some compelling evidence that Relationship Enhancement communication training is an effective intervention for secondary prevention of domestic violence. Subsequent research has further demonstrated secondary prevention benefits from domestic violence prevention group work (Schwartz & Waldo, 1999, 2003; Waldo, Kerne, & Van Horne Kerne, 2007).

Tertiary Prevention. Tertiary prevention focuses on preventing an existing problem from causing other problems. An example of the authors' use of Relationship Enhancement communication training as a tertiary prevention intervention with patients in a state mental hospital was described earlier in this book (Waldo & Harman, 1999). This was a preexperimental posttest-only study. The training was provided for hospital patients, and the impact of the training was assessed afterward by the hospital staff. The training was not intended to cure the serious mental disorders that necessitated hospitalizing many of the patients but, instead, was intended to help prevent those mental disorders from causing withdrawal and interpersonal conflicts that isolate patients from each other and the staff. Relationship Enhancement training was offered to 20 patients. Qualitative analysis of staff members' perceptions of the impact of the training suggested that it had biological (reduced self-mutilation), psychological (improved ability to identify emotional issues), and social (improved roommate relations) benefits for patients. The results suggest that additional research on the tertiary prevention benefits of Relationship Enhancement training with hospitalized patients is warranted.

Service Delivery

Once primary, secondary, and tertiary interventions have been found to prevent the epidemiology of biological, psychological, and social problems, the next step is to identify the most effective and efficient ways in which those intervention services can be delivered. Examples of service delivery studies in relation to the

(Continued)

(Continued)

research described above could be studying the use of computer programs to provide training in Relationship Enhancement skills for college roommates; examining if Relationship Enhancement provided by former participants in domestic violence prevention groups is as effective as training offered by professionals for preventing the reoccurrence of domestic violence; and testing the efficacy of weekly Relationship Enhancement training as opposed to monthly training for hospitalized patients. An example of the authors' service delivery research focused on a train-the-trainer model for delivering Relationship Enhancement cross-cultural communication skills training to teachers. Two experimental studies indicated that preservice teachers made significant improvements in their ability to communicate in multicultural situations and appropriately address prejudice following participation in multicultural Relationship Enhancement communication skills workshops (Adams et al., 2003; Arizaga, Bauman, Waldo, & Castellanos, 2005). The workshops were led by professors and graduate students. They were held in university classrooms and attended by preservice teachers as part of their teacher education program. While this system worked well for preservice teachers, it could not be practically implemented statewide for in-service teachers, many of whom lived and worked far from universities and who did not have time for extended involvement in training. Also, there were not enough professors and graduate students available to offer training to all the teachers who could benefit from participating. To address this service delivery problem, a train-the-trainer model titled "Supporting Teachers Supporting Students" was implemented and evaluated (Kenny, Waldo, Warter, & Barton, 2002, p. 736). The model involved bringing one or two staff members (teachers or other school personnel) from schools throughout the state to a centrally located training facility. There the school staff members learned how to use Relationship Enhancement communication in multicultural situations. They also learned how to lead training in Relationship Enhancement communication and other preventive interventions for their colleagues back in their schools. They then returned to their schools and led the training for their colleagues. This service delivery system allowed training of place-bound teachers across the state. In 1 year, 115 trained leaders offered Relationship Enhancement and other prevention-oriented trainings for more than 1,150 of their colleagues back in their schools. It was estimated that the 1,150 participants would employ what they learned with approximately 35,000 students that they served in their schools. The intervention cost $135,000, which came to less than $4 per student. Evaluation of the service delivery model was limited to a posttest assessment of staff participants' experience. Ninety-two percent of the participants' rated the training the leaders offered as useful or very/extremely useful and indicated that they were satisfied or extremely satisfied with the training experience. There is room for extensive improvement of this study, including use of a true experimental design and measures of participants' acquisition of knowledge and skills. More important, the impact the program has on students' biological, psychological, and social development needs to be assessed. The study does demonstrate that a train-the-trainers' service delivery model can efficiently reach a large number of participants and be well received.

Activity

Consider an area of prevention that is important to you. Identify several articles evaluating preventive interventions related to this area and use them to answer the following questions.

- To what extent are the principles described by Nation et al. (2003) in evidence for the interventions described in the articles? Consider each principle separately. What principles have the most evidence? The least? Why might this be? What types of additional information would be helpful in making your evaluation of the programs?
- To what extent are the standards proposed by the Society for Prevention Research (Flay et al., 2005) in evidence for the interventions described in the articles? What domains have the most evidence? The least? Why might this be? What types of additional information would be helpful in making your evaluation of the programs?
- Where do your selected interventions fall within the classification matrix? Using the classification matrix, identify what other types of research may be helpful in understanding this area of prevention.

4 Selecting and Implementing Evidence-Based Programs

I n the previous chapter, we presented general information pertaining to the characteristics of impactful programs, a set of standards available for identifying programs as efficacious, effective, and ready for dissemination, and a classification matrix for categorizing research programs. In this chapter, we offer suggestions for selecting and implementing evidence-based prevention programs. First, we provide guidance for identifying appropriate programs by highlighting several popular registries of evidence-based programs. Next, we describe the process for evaluating your own circumstances and needs and selecting a program that meets those needs. We pay particular attention to issues pertaining to implementing and evaluating the selected programs.

Identifying Evidence-Based Programs

In Book 7 of this series, *Program Development and Evaluation in Prevention*, Conyne identified a number of processes that are critical to developing an evidence-based approach to the implementation of a prevention effort. He emphasized the three Cs: community, collaboration, and cultural relevance, which are essential to effective prevention efforts. Without the engagement of the community and maintaining relevance of the community culture and mores to the efforts being proposed, there will be little buy-in of constituents who need to be engaged in the process. Similarly, collaboration among the members of the community, the prevention proposers, and the agencies and personnel who will be conducting the prevention efforts is essential. Finally, being certain to maintain awareness and respect of the cultural heritage and traditions of the intended audience is critical for establishing an influential prevention program. Awareness of and attention to each of these three Cs is necessary for a program to be as impactful as planned and anticipated.

As indicated by Conyne (2012) and reflected in the systems of evidence-based evaluation described below, it is critical that there be a focus on research efficacy and clinical utility. While it is essential that each program being considered for implementation have a strong research basis and be held to high standards of peer review assessing the quality of the program, it must also be highly relevant and of considerable utility. Prevention programs are expensive and must be justifiable to warrant the funding required—in other words, they must have clinical utility.

A number of popular registries exist that compile lists of evidence-based programs. In this section, we describe several of those resources that may be useful for mental health workers in identifying prevention programs, the National Registry of Evidence-Based Programs and Practices (NREPP), the What Works Clearinghouse, the Promising Practices Network, Social Programs That Work, and Blueprints for Violence Prevention.

National Registry of Evidence-Based Programs and Practices

Focus Areas

- Mental health promotion
- Mental health treatment
- Substance abuse prevention
- Substance abuse treatment

Website: http://nrepp.samhsa.gov/

Summary

NREPP is an online registry of interventions related to mental health promotion and treatment and substance abuse prevention and treatment. NREPP is operated by the Substance Abuse and Mental Health Services Administration (SAMHSA) under the U.S. Department of Health and Human Services (U.S. DHHS). As of March 2012, there are more than 220 interventions included on the registry. Each intervention has been assessed by independent reviewers and must meet minimum criteria to be included in the registry. NREPP is a voluntary system; intervention developers must submit their programs for possible inclusion in the registry, and only those who meet the criteria will be included. These criteria relate to (a) quality of research and (b) readiness for dissemination. With regard to quality of research, programs are evaluated across the following six subcategories:

1. Reliability of measures
2. Validity of measures
3. Intervention fidelity
4. Missing data and attrition
5. Potential confounding variables
6. Appropriateness of analysis

With regard to readiness for dissemination, programs are evaluated across the following three subcategories:

1. Availability of implementation materials

2. Availability of training and support resources

3. Availability of quality assurance procedures

Detailed information related to how programs are evaluated across these criteria, including the scoring rubrics that are used by reviewers, is provided on the NREPP website.

The NREPP website includes a user-friendly interface for identifying applicable programs. Users can browse or search by keywords, and results can be narrowed down by targeted age, area of interest (e.g., mental health promotion), intervention setting (e.g., workplace), outcome of interest (e.g., alcohol use), race/ethnicity, geographic location, gender, and level of implementation/replication. For each program included in the registry, a full intervention summary is provided. This summary includes descriptive information, outcomes, ratings on the quality of research and readiness for dissemination criteria, and detailed costs of the program.

One major strength of this website is the high degree of transparency of the evaluation process. The format also allows users to easily evaluate the relative strengths and weaknesses of different programs. Another advantage of the site is the emphasis on readiness for dissemination. For users who wish to identify and implement prevention programs, it is important to know that a given program is available for purchase and that an adequate degree of training and support is available. Overall, NREPP is an excellent source for obtaining clear and comprehensive information on evidence-based prevention programs.

What Works Clearinghouse

Focus Area

- Educational outcomes

Website: http://ies.ed.gov/ncee/wwc/

Summary

The What Works Clearinghouse is an online resource for information about interventions related to improving educational outcomes, including academic, personal, and social development. The What Works Clearinghouse is operated by the U.S. Department of Education's Institute of Education Sciences (IES). The What Works Clearinghouse provides intervention reports and practice guides. *Intervention reports* summarize the research findings related to specific interventions and policies. Interventions are evaluated according to the quality of available evidence, and detailed criteria are available for download from the website.

Practice guides summarize recommendations related to a particular topic, such as dropout prevention, with an assessment of the level of evidence (i.e., minimal, moderate, strong) supporting each recommendation. As of March 2012, there were more than 250 intervention reports and 19 practice guides available over 15 broad topic areas.

Users of the website may browse for interventions by topic area or search by intervention name. Under each topic area, results may be narrowed by the outcome domain (e.g., social outcomes), grade level, population (i.e., general vs. special education), effectiveness rating (i.e., positive, potentially positive, no discernible effects), extent of evidence (i.e., small, medium to large, not rated), delivery method (e.g., small group), and program type (e.g., curriculum). For each intervention, an "improvement index" is provided, which indicates the change in a student's percentile rank that would be expected due to the intervention. Programs can be easily sorted by the improvement index, effectiveness rating, and extent of evidence rating.

The intervention reports provide detailed summaries of the research evidence of a given program, including a program description, a summary of the research supporting the program, an evaluation of the effectiveness of the program, and cost information. The intervention reports are well formatted and easily printable to be shared with other stakeholders assisting in the decision-making process.

A strength of The What Works Clearinghouse is the large number of reviewed interventions; however, many of these interventions are focused on improving academic outcomes. Therefore, this website may be less useful to counselors, psychologists, social workers, and other mental health workers who work outside of educational contexts.

Promising Practices Network

Focus Areas

- Healthy and safe children
- Children ready for school
- Children succeeding in school
- Strong families

Website: http://www.promisingpractices.net/

Summary

The Promising Practices Network is an online registry of programs that have been identified as improving the lives of children and families. The network is operated by the RAND Corporation. As of March 2012, the website included approximately 80 interventions categorized as "proven" or "promising" in one of four focus areas: (1) healthy and safe children,

(2) children ready for school, (3) children succeeding in school, and (4) strong families. Programs are designated proven or promising based on criteria in six areas:

1. Type of outcomes affected

2. Substantial effect size

3. Statistically significant

4. Inclusion of comparison groups

5. Adequacy of sample size

6. Availability of program evaluation documentation

Proven programs are required to meet a higher level of evidence than promising programs; however, the requirements to meet either of these criteria appear to be less rigorous than those of NREPP or the What Works Clearinghouse. An additional approximately 100 programs are listed on the website as being "screened." Screened programs have not been evaluated by Promising Programs Network personnel but have been identified by other trustworthy organizations as being effective.

Users can browse to find interventions by focus area, age of child, type of setting (e.g., preschool), type of service (e.g., mentoring), type of outcome addressed, and level of evidence (i.e., proven or promising). For each reviewed program, a summary page is available that provides a program overview, description of participants, evaluation methods, key evaluation findings, program cost, and other issues to consider. The summary provides a readable overview of the evidence supporting the positive outcomes for a given program.

Overall, this website will be helpful in identifying programs specifically targeted to children and their families. Drawbacks of the registry include relatively weak inclusion criteria, and a large number of "screened" programs that are included on the site but not reviewed by Promising Programs Network staff.

Social Programs That Work

Focus Areas

- Prenatal/early childhood
- K–12 education
- Postsecondary education
- Teen pregnancy prevention
- Crime/violence prevention
- Housing/homelessness

- Employment and welfare
- Substance abuse/treatment
- Obesity prevention/treatment
- Mental Health
- Health care financing and delivery
- International development

Website: http://evidencebasedprograms.org/wordpress/

Summary

Social Programs That Work is an online registry of programs that have been identified as providing substantial and prolonged benefits across a wide spectrum of social policy areas. The site is operated by the Coalition for Evidence-Based Policy, a nonprofit, nonpartisan group, and it focuses on programs that have been evaluated with randomized controlled trials. As of March 2012, the website included approximately 40 interventions across all policy areas. Of these, 9 programs are identified as "top tier," and 5 are identified as "near top tier." The standards for earning these labels are outlined on the Social Programs That Work website and include criteria in the following broad areas:

- Overall study design
- Equivalency of treatment and control groups over the course of the study
- Outcome measures
- Reporting of the intervention effects

Top tier and near top tier programs have been determined to demonstrate sizable and sustained positive outcomes. Top tier programs also must have a high-quality replication study that also demonstrated sizable and sustained results. The remainder of the programs listed on the website have not yet met the requirements to be labeled top tier or near top tier programs but have been identified by Social Programs That Work staff as being promising.

Programs are organized under the 12 broad policy areas listed above. For each intervention listed, a summary of the relevant research findings is provided. This summary provides a description of the intervention, the evidence of effectiveness, and a discussion of the study quality. The website lacks some of the sorting and filtering options available in other registries but is still very easy to use.

Overall, the website is a valuable resource for identifying the relatively limited number of studies that have demonstrated sustained, positive results over time. However, because the bar is set quite high, there may be many areas of prevention work with no recommended programs. For example, under the topic area "mental health," there is only one intervention listed—Group

Cognitive Behavioral Therapy—and this program was deemed promising for preventing depression. Prevention workers looking for interventions to prevent other types of mental health problems would need to consult other sources.

Blueprints for Violence Prevention

Focus Areas

- Violence prevention
- Drug abuse prevention

Website: http://www.colorado.edu/cspv/blueprints/

Summary

Blueprints for Violence Prevention is an online registry of programs that have been identified as effective in preventing violence or drug abuse. The registry is operated by the Center for the Study and Prevention of Violence at the University of Colorado. As of March 2012, the website included 11 model programs and 22 promising programs. Programs are evaluated on criteria in three main categories:

1. Evidence of effect with a strong research design

2. Sustained effects

3. Replication

Model programs must meet the criteria in all three of these areas, and promising programs must meet criteria in the first area. The review process also takes into account (a) evidence that the intervention produces desirable changes in relevant risk and protective factors and (b) cost–benefit considerations. A detailed explanation of the evaluation criteria is available on the Blueprints website.

Users can browse lists of interventions at either level of effectiveness (i.e., model or promising) or can use the interactive program selection feature to search for interventions by (a) level of intervention (e.g., community, family, individual), (b) target age, (c) audience, and (d) type of program (e.g., social skills training, mentoring). For each intervention, a summary is provided with information on the targeted audience, program content, and outcomes. Each of the model programs also has a short video segment describing the program and its positive outcomes. Overall, the Blueprints website is a helpful resource for identifying programs for violence and drug abuse prevention. Because the evaluation criteria are rigorous, the number of programs described on the website is quite small.

Summary

In this section, we have described several popular online registries for identifying evidence-based prevention programs. To appeal to a broad readership, we have focused on registries that cover multiple areas of prevention. We hope that at least one of the registries described to this point will address the prevention areas that are important to you. Note that there are also other websites that focus on narrower categories of evidence-based prevention, such as the Suicide Prevention Resource Center (http://www.sprc.org/).

In using registries to identify potential prevention programs, keep in mind that the higher the bar is set in terms of evidence, fewer programs will be able to meet that criteria. Ideally, for a given prevention area and context, an appropriate program will be available that has met the highest standards of effectiveness. However, this may not always (or even often) be the case. Just because a program has not been included in the highest tier of a registry does not mean that it cannot be effective. There are a number of reasons why a program may not appear on a registry. It may be a newly developed program or a program that has not undergone a thorough-enough evaluation. In this case, it is possible that the program is very effective, but we don't have enough evidence to know it yet. Note that high-quality evaluations take time, especially when long-term follow-up and/or replications are required. On the other hand, it could be the case that a program has been evaluated and has not demonstrated positive outcomes. When identifying potential prevention programs (from a registry or from another source), it is important to take the next step and read the peer-reviewed publications of a program's impact. This review will help you determine whether the program has produced the types of outcomes that you desire and will help you get a sense for how well the study conditions match your own circumstances. In the next section, we describe additional considerations for selecting an appropriate prevention program.

Selecting Evidence-Based Programs

There are many factors that influence the selection of an evidence-based prevention program. Since many readers will be affiliated with schools, community agencies, mental health facilities, and other similar settings, it is important to be highly professional and pragmatic in selecting a prevention program. Thus, we encourage you to go through a selection process that systematically examines important considerations and leads into an evaluation of prevention practices at your site. There are several steps we recommend. These are (a) determining the need for a prevention program, (b) deciding on the targeted population and identifying program goals, (c) selecting the program, (d) implementing and evaluating, and (e) sharing results. In this section, we use the example of "Claire" to walk through these steps for selecting an evidence-based program. For the sake of simplicity, we discuss Claire as an individual prevention worker, but it is desirable (and in many cases necessary) for the steps to be carried out by a committed team of prevention professionals.

Determining the Need for a Prevention Program

Claire had been the counselor at her middle school for several weeks. New to the job, she was still learning her way around the school and was becoming aware of issues and concerns that seemed to be important to address through the counselor's office. One was that there was a considerable amount of rough-housing in the halls, and it often seemed to be serious enough to be called bullying or harassment. She decided that a program for preventing bullying would be appropriate and began steps to find out what programs were available.

The first step to conducting a prevention program is to determine whether there is a need for the program. What evidence exists that there is a problem that needs to be fixed? Is the issue relevant and important? Is the problem an individual issue or a systemic concern?

Claire met with her principal, and she suggested that there may be a problem but that it would be important to know how extensive the concern was, how many students were involved, and whether it was something others saw as an issue. Claire reviewed websites to determine what preexisting resources are available to assess bullying in schools.

A primary way to evaluate need is to collect data. In Chapter 2, we discussed different types of data that can be collected. One particularly relevant section of that discussion pertains to needs assessment. As a recap, needs assessment provides evidence regarding what needs a population has and how well those needs are being met. An important aspect of needs assessment is triangulation. That is, information should be collected from a variety of sources to help ensure that multiple perspectives on the problem are captured. Data can be collected using a variety of methods, such as surveys, focus groups, informal conversations, observations, and examination of existing records. Goals of the information-collecting stage may include the following:

- Identifying the extent of the problem from multiple perspectives
- Finding out what has been done in the past and what is currently being done to address the problem
- Determining how others think the problem should be addressed
- Evaluating what level of resources are available to address the problem

A well thought out data collection plan can help prevention workers attain these goals. In the case of Claire, she may develop a data collection plan that includes the following components:

- Surveys of students, teachers, and parents
- Focus groups with students

- Informal conversations with administrators and other adults at school
- Observations of aggressive behavior in various locations around the school
- Evaluation of school records, such as the number of discipline incidents reported in the past year

In this section, we expand on one aspect of the data collection plan: the use of surveys. Administering a set of surveys tailored for different audiences (e.g., students, teachers, administrators, and parents) would be appropriate. Our experience with evaluating bullying is that the surveys cannot be targeted to students alone. All members of the school community will likely have some experience with the problem, and their perspectives are valuable. In our bullying prevention efforts with schools, we find that students generally report about twice as much bullying as teachers. Students report that bullying occurs in more situations and locations than teachers report, and students indicate that teachers follow through with consequences for bullying far less often than teachers report. We provide this example to show that it is important to gauge differences in perceptions of the problem before beginning a prevention program. Addressing these differences, if present, is an important part of the prevention plan. If teachers believe that bullying is not a substantial problem, they will likely lack buy-in to a prevention program, and these attitudes may influence the implementation and success of the program.

Claire will need to develop survey questions or find a preexisting survey to meet her needs. If high-quality preexisting surveys exist, it may be easier to use them than to create a new survey. It is also desirable to use survey questions that have been previously evaluated for clarity and appropriateness. A variety of resources are available for locating preexisting surveys. In Claire's case, she may decide to develop a survey using the compendium of assessment tools provided by the Centers for Disease Control and Prevention, *Measuring Violence-Related Attitudes, Behaviors, and Influences Among Youths: A Compendium of Assessment Tools* (Dahlberg, Toal, Swahn, & Behrens, 2005). This resource is available as a free download at http://www.cdc.gov/ncipc/pub-res/measure.htm. Another helpful resource is the Inventory for Aggression Assessment, a service of the Violence Institute of New Jersey at UMDNJ (http://vinst.umdnj.edu/VAID/query.asp). This webpage provides summary information on several hundred measures of aggression, violence, bullying, and other related topics. The site includes a searchable interface, and users can filter assessments by topic area, age range/grade level, and information source (e.g., student, parent), among others.

After selecting survey(s) to use, a plan for distribution should be developed. Two important considerations are (1) distributing the materials in such a way as to increase the likelihood that respondents will respond and

(2) if possible, reducing the burden of entering the data from completed surveys. Regarding response rates, some circumstances will make obtaining high participation in the survey easier than others. For example, teachers and students may be surveyed at school during a designated time, rendering data collection relatively easy. Obtaining parent surveys will likely be more difficult. Multiple forms of communication may be necessary to reach out to parents, and even so, a high rate of participation may not be possible. Prevention workers developing a data collection plan should consider different ways of reaching out to the targeted community in consultation with representatives from that group to help obtain a reasonable response rate. Should surveys be mailed? Conducted online? Are there community events (e.g., back to school night, parent–teacher conferences) that would be appropriate for reaching participants?

Another data collection consideration pertains to entering the information so it can be analyzed. Entering a large number of surveys into a spreadsheet by hand can be enormously time-intensive. Online surveys, if possible, are a preferred option. With the increasing popularity of smartphones and other handheld devices that can connect to the Internet (and thus online surveys), it seems likely that more data collection activities will shift online in the future. Keep in mind that regardless of the data collection method(s), confidentiality issues must be considered.

Once the data have been collected, they must be analyzed. For many applications, a basic description of the data (e.g., means and standard deviations) will be sufficient. Do results of the data collection support the idea that there is a problem? What aspects of the problem appear to be most salient? For whom? Investigating results by subgroup will likely be important. For example, Claire may want to report the average amount of bullying reported by boys and girls separately and for each grade separately. The goal of data analysis is to obtain a clear picture that helps point to the way forward with prevention efforts.

Deciding on the Targeted Population and Identifying Program Goals

Once a need has been determined, identifying the population to be targeted for the prevention efforts is critical. In the case of preventing bullying in a school, who will participate in prevention activities? Should the program target students directly? Or is it better to work with teachers to help them intervene in problem situations? Or should parenting groups be formed to help parents individually assist their children? Or should all of these activities be included in the prevention program? Based on the results of the data collection, one or more targeted populations may be identified. It is also important to factor in the level of resources available for the prevention effort. When significant resources are available, a more comprehensive program will be possible. When resources are limited, the prevention team must think pragmatically and prioritize to target the population that is most likely to benefit from a prevention program.

Claire was surprised by the results of the survey she conducted at the school. Most teachers reported that there was not much of a problem and that any concerns were primarily a few students who had not learned the social skills to manage teasing. Most students reported that there was a good deal of bullying occurring and that they wanted to feel safer at school. Several students reported that the bullying was extensive and caused them to have trouble academically.

In this situation, several simultaneous interventions may be appropriate. For teachers, it may be appropriate to initiate a program to provide them with the definition of bullying, common examples of bullying and situations where it may occur, and appropriate actions for teachers to take to prevent and respond to bullying.

For students, a general bullying prevention program that provides a universal psychoeducational learning program will be appropriate to teach all students effective problem solving, conflict management, and interpersonal social skills. In addition to this universal program, a second level of prevention that addresses the needs of students at elevated risk for chronic involvement in bullying is also warranted.

For each type of intervention, Claire should develop specific, measurable objectives that she would like to attain by the end of the preventive intervention. For example, for teachers, she may want to see increases in awareness of bullying and confidence in how to handle bullying situations, as measured by a pretest and a posttest. She may want to observe a decrease in the number of bullying incidents reported by students at the end of the program and a higher level of school connectedness.

Selecting the Program

Once the targeted population has been determined, the next step is to select a program that matches the current circumstances, needs, and targeted population. The online registries described in the previous section are a helpful resource for locating programs. In selecting a program, prevention workers should consider the following questions:

- How closely do the outcomes of the program align with the results I would like to see?
- In terms of population, sociocultural context, and other relevant factors, how similar was the program to my circumstances?
- What level of resources will be needed to implement the program? What are the costs of the program? Will this be feasible given my current circumstances?

- How much information, training, and support are available for those implementing the program? Is the program manual detailed enough? Is the level of training and support sufficient for my needs?

It is important to evaluate programs on the characteristics described by Conyne in Book 7 of this series. The program should engage the community, require a collaborative approach to implementation and application, and be culturally relevant to the populations being served. Furthermore, they should have a strong basis of evaluation and validation and should be relevant—that is, have clinical utility. In Claire's situation, she determined that programs focused on two target audiences—teachers and students— were appropriate.

For teachers, a number of programs have been shown to increase teachers' awareness of the problem, enhance their commitment to improving the classroom and school climate, and increase their sense of efficacy for working with bullying problems (Orpinas & Horne, 2006). The Olweus Bully Prevention Program is identified by the Blueprints for Violence Prevention Program as an evidence-based program that has a strong teacher prevention component (Limber, 2004). Another program for reducing bullying with an emphasis on developing teacher awareness, knowledge, and efficacy is the Bully Busters Program (Horne, Bartolomucci, & Newman-Carlson, 2004). This program has evidence of impact on reducing school bullying and improved teacher agency (Horne, Orpinas, Newman-Carlson, & Bartolomucci, 2004), but it has not yet experienced the thorough evaluation required to be defined as an evidence-based prevention program.

For students, the Olweus Program (Limber, 2004) has also been defined as an evidence-based approach to the prevention of bullying in schools. The work has primarily been done with schools in Scandinavian countries, including Finland, Sweden, and Norway. Claire and other educators will have to determine the suitability of the program for the student population they may serve in their schools. The Bully Busters Program also serves as a general psychoeducational approach to teaching students effective social skills and problem-solving methods to promote healthier school climates.

A second level of prevention may also be called for with Claire's school. She may find it helpful to try out a program that more specifically targets persistent forms of bullying. An example of this program is the Method of Shared Concern (Rigby, 2009). In this approach, students who have been actively engaged in bullying or have been the target of bullying are attended to through individual approaches to help define the problem area and then establish appropriate alternative ways of managing conflict. The program has been demonstrated to be quite successful and has led to the prevention of future bullying in schools in that students who have participated have reduced their bullying and aggression. Furthermore, having students engage in the program results in modeling of behavior change that influences other students (Rigby, 2009).

Adapting Evidence-Based Programs to Other Cultures

One area that may present special challenges with regard to the selecting and implementing of evidence-based prevention programs relates to adapting programs to other cultures. In Chapter 2, we discussed issues pertaining to the external validity of prevention programs. What should a prevention worker do if evidence-based programs have been shown to work, but only with participants or in settings that are quite different from their own targeted population or setting? The issue of adapting evidence-based prevention programs for other populations and settings is a difficult issue that has received increasing attention. While researchers and practitioners are increasingly called on to study and implement evidence-based prevention, it is also true that that prevention cannot be "one-size-fits-all." Modifications to evidence-based programs may be necessary to enhance their relevance to the new population or setting.

One challenge in cultural adaption of evidence-based interventions is to strike a balance between fidelity to the successful components of the intervention and adaption to meet the contextual characteristics of the new context. Poulsen et al. (2010) discussed adapting an evidence-based HIV prevention intervention to a new setting in rural Kenya. They utilized a systematic process to determine which HIV prevention program was most appropriate and what modifications were necessary. First, they conducted a community needs assessment. Based on that needs assessment, they reviewed evidence-based prevention programs that fit the specific needs of that community. After selecting a program, they carefully adapted the program—originally designed in the United States—to meet the cultural context of rural Kenya. Finally, the researchers pilot tested the adapted intervention and implemented it, monitoring its effectiveness throughout. The study results provided additional support for the HIV prevention program. The authors highlighted the importance of conducting adaptations with a multidisciplinary team with strong community representation.

If you decide to select a prevention program that has been implemented successfully only with populations or in settings that are dissimilar to your own, we recommend that you carefully consider how these contextual differences may affect the results of the intervention. We suggest that you assemble a team to assist in identifying areas that may need to be modified and ways that these modifications can be implemented. This team should include strong representation of the members of the targeted audience. As stated before, the process of adaptation consists of a balancing act between remaining faithful to the original program and making changes to aspects of the program that may be inappropriate or irrelevant to the new population or setting.

In summary, for prevention to be effective, it needs to address variables that are salient within the sociocultural context in which it is implemented, employ intervention strategies that are accepted within that context, and be delivered through available service systems. Each of these areas can vary widely in different cultural contexts. It is critical that preventionists take these variations into account when translating prevention from one culture to another. Probably, the single best tool in making that translation is close collaboration with representatives from the target audience.

Implementing and Evaluating the Program

The next step is implementing the program. However, before the program begins, an evaluation plan should be in place. The evaluation plan should be linked to the program goals that were defined in the previous steps. Program goals can be divided into several categories: outcome objectives, impact objectives, and process objectives. Outcome objectives refer to the ultimate goals of the program, such as reducing the number of bullying and victimization incidents reported by students by a certain percent. Impact objectives refer to intermediate goals that lead to the overall goals of the project, such as an increase in student-reported use of conflict resolution skills. Process objectives refer to how the implementation of the program is carried out, such as the percentage of teachers who attended the intervention sessions (i.e., coverage) and how closely the implementation followed the program manual (i.e., delivery).

With regard to implementation, some prevention programs may be brief. The teacher intervention may occur as a 1-day event, for example. Others may be more extensive. The universal bullying prevention program in which all students in a school are exposed to the program may take place over the entire school year. Another program developed for reducing bullying in high schools, Empowering Teen Peers to Prevent Bullying: The Bully Busters Program for High Schools (Horne et al., 2012) begins with a summer training program for seniors in high school in which they are taught peer leadership skills. The seniors then work with first-year (ninth-grade) students throughout the school year under the supervision of school counselors. The Method of Shared Concern process occurs during the year as needed by the counselors.

The evaluation process often will include a postassessment of surveys or instruments that were used in the process of determining whether a problem existed that warranted a prevention effort to be offered. In addition, it is usually critical that the prevention facilitator explores other avenues of information. For example, in one of our bullying prevention efforts with a middle school, the data indicated that changes had occurred for teachers—they had increased levels of knowledge, skills, and had a considerably more positive sense of efficacy for managing the concerns of bullying within the school. Student surveys, however, did not indicate a significant decrease in bullying within the school (Bell, Raczynski, & Horne, 2010). We conducted a qualitative process interviewing students to determine what explanation they would have for the teachers becoming more confident and skilled while students reported little change. The interviewed students explained several causes for the discrepancy of outcomes. First, they said they had reported more bullying at the end of the program because they had a clearer idea of what bullying was at the end of the program. In the beginning, they were not really sure of what was bullying and what wasn't. By the end, they were quite familiar and reported it more frequently. Second, they indicated that about half of the teachers were not implementing the program properly. Although the teachers participated in the in-service training, and all reported to be implementing the program in their classes, the students reported that some teachers indicated that they thought the program was unimportant. Specifically, students stated that teachers used the time devoted to the program for academic activities instead, likely because teacher evaluations were based on students' standardized subject matter scores and not the students behavior or social competence. We offer this example to underscore that it is important to seek out multiple perspectives on the intervention both during and after the program has taken place.

Sharing Results

Once a program has been implemented, it is important to share the results of the efforts, regardless of the outcome. If the efforts have resulted in improvement, it is desirable to share this information so that greater support and resources may be provided for the effort. If, on the other hand, the results were less impressive, it is important that participants be aware of the outcomes and explore possibilities for how to improve the delivery or execution of services for future programs. In a bullying prevention program, it is critical that the students, faculty, parents, and administrators are all apprised of the outcome and become engaged in activities to explore more effective prevention services in the future. As was mentioned in Chapter 1 with regard to clinical skills in working with clients, it is important to not blame the facilitator or the participants for failing to have positive outcomes. In our experience, we find that we need to examine contextual factors such as insufficient dosage, competing experiences, failure of administrators to follow through on support, and a myriad other possible events that could have marred the implementation process.

This example with Claire has focused on preventing bullying in schools. However, the steps that we have outlined here may be applied to many other prevention areas and settings with minimal modification. It is especially important to remember to the following:

1. Clearly define the problem. Seek input from those who are affected by the problem you are trying to address.

2. Realistically evaluate the level of resources and support that are available. Ask for support from those who allocate resources while you are still in the early planning phases. Without strong administrative backing, it can be very difficult to produce impactful results, even with a prevention program that has worked in other settings. The support of "the powers that be" can be a make-it-or-break-it factor when it comes to obtaining positive impact.

Summary

This chapter has focused on practical strategies for prevention workers to identify, select, implement, and evaluate prevention programs. We have emphasized selecting programs from registries of evidence-based programs, if applicable. Several popular and easy to use registries exist, and they may be a helpful resource for identifying evidence-based programs. After establishing the need for a program and developing prevention goals, prevention workers should select a program that matches the needs and preferences of the targeted audience. In some cases, the program may need to be adapted to make it more relevant and appropriate to the new setting. Throughout the implementation, it is important to evaluate the program and share these results. A key aspect of evidence-based prevention is generating new knowledge about the outcomes of prevention programs to inform future efforts.

Activity

Identify an area of prevention that is of interest to you. Locate evidence-based prevention programs addressing this area of prevention using at least two of the registries described in this chapter. Answer the following questions:

- How easily were you able to navigate each registry? Which registry was the easiest to navigate? Which provided the most helpful and comprehensive information regarding evidence-based programs in your area of interest?
- How many prevention programs in your area of interest were you able to locate using the registries? Of these, how many appear to be appropriate for your current or future plans for prevention work? In what ways were they a good match for your needs? In what ways were they not? What other sources of information will you use to supplement online registries in identifying prevention programs that are appropriate for your circumstances?
- In planning your current or future prevention work, what types of information will you collect from the targeted audience and others to determine the need for a prevention program? What types of information will you collect to evaluate how well the prevention program is working?

References _____

Adams, E., Waldo, M., Steiner, R., Mayfield, R., Ackerlind, S., & Castellanos, L. (2003). Creating peace by confronting prejudice: Examining the effects of a multicultural communication skills group intervention. *International Journal for the Advancement of Counseling, 25,* 281–291.

American Counseling Association. (2005). *Code of ethics.* Alexandria, VA: Author.

American Psychological Association. (2005). *Policy statement on evidence-based practice in psychology.* Retrieved from http://www.apa.org/practice/resources/ evidence/evidence-based-statement.pdf

American Psychological Association Presidential Task Force on Evidence-Based Practice. (2006). Evidence-based practice in psychology. *American Psychologist, 61,* 271–285. doi:10.1037/0003-066X.61.4.271

Arizaga, M., Bauman, S., Waldo, M., & Castellanos, L. (2005). Multicultural sensitivity and interpersonal skill training for pre-service teachers. *Journal of Humanistic Counseling, Education, and Development, 44,* 198–208.

Bell, C., Raczynski, K. A., & Horne, A. M. (2010). Bully Busters abbreviated: Evaluation of a group-based bully intervention and prevention program. *Group Dynamics: Theory, Research, and Practice, 14,* 257–267.

Bronfenbrenner, U. (1979). *The ecology of human development.* Cambridge, MA: Harvard University Press.

Caplan, G. (1964). *Principles of preventive psychiatry.* New York, NY: Basic Books.

Cohen J. (1994, April). The power of counseling: For better or worse? *Australian Family Physician, 4,* 560–562.

Conyne, R. K (2012). *Program development and evaluation in prevention* [Monograph]. Thousand Oaks, CA: Sage.

Conyne, R. K., Horne, A. M., & Raczynski, K. A. (2012). *Prevention in psychology: An introduction to the prevention practice kit* [Monograph]. Thousand Oaks, CA: Sage.

Cook, T. D., & Campbell, D. T. (1979). *Quasi experimentation: Design and analytical issues for field settings.* Chicago, IL: Rand McNally.

Dahlberg, L. L., Toal, S. B., Swahn, M., & Behrens, C. B. (2005). *Measuring violence-related attitudes, behaviors, and influences among youths: A compendium of assessment tools* (2nd ed.). Atlanta, GA: Centers for Disease Control and Prevention, National Center for Injury Prevention and Control.

Duncan, B. L., & Miller, S. D. (2006). Treatment manuals do not improve outcomes. In J. C. Norcross, L. E. Beutler, & R. F. Levant (Eds.), *Evidence-based practices in mental health: Debate and dialogue on the fundamental questions* (pp. 140–149). Washington, DC: American Psychological Association.

Flay, B. R., Biglan, A., Boruch, R. F., Castro, F. G., Gottfredson, D., Kellam, S., . . . Ji, P. (2005). Standards of evidence: Criteria for efficacy, effectiveness, and dissemination. *Prevention Science, 6,* 151–175. doi:10.1007/s11121-005-5553-y

Gelso, C. J., & Fretz, B. R. (1992). *Counseling psychology.* San Diego, CA: Harcourt Brace Jovanovich.

Goodman, R. M., Wandersman, A., Chinman, M., & Imm, P. (1996). An ecological assessment of community-based interventions for prevention and health promotion: Approaches to measuring community coalitions. *American Journal of Community Psychology, 24*(1), 33–61.

Gordon, R. (1987). An operational classification of disease prevention. In J. A. Sternberg & M. M. Silverman (Eds.), *Preventing mental disorders* (pp. 20–26). Rockville, MD: U.S. Department of Health and Human Services.

Guerney, B. (1977). *Relationship enhancement: Skill-training programs for therapy, problem prevention, and enrichment.* San Francisco, CA: Jossey-Bass.

Hage, S. M., Romano, J. L., Conyne, R., Kenny, M., Matthews, C., Schwartz, J. P., & Waldo, M. (2007). Best practice guidelines on prevention practice, research, training, and social advocacy for psychologists. *The Counseling Psychologist, 35,* 493–566.

Henry, W. P., Strupp, H. H., Butler, S. F., Schacht, T. E., & Binder, J. L. (1993). Effects of training in time-limited dynamic psychotherapy: Changes in therapist behavior. *Journal of Consulting and Clinical Psychology, 61,* 434–440.

Heppner, P. P., Kivlighan, D. M., & Wampold, B. E. (2008). *Research design in counseling* (3rd ed.). Belmont, CA: Thomson, Brooks/Cole.

Horne, A. M., Bartolomucci, C. L., & Newman-Carlson, D. (2003). *Bully Busters: A teacher's manual for helping bullies, victims, and bystanders (Grades K-5).* Champaign, IL: Research Press.

Horne, A., Nitza, A., Dobias, B., Jolliff, D., Raczynski, K., & Voors, W. (2012.) *Empowering teen peers to prevent bullying: The Bully Busters Program for high schools.* Champaign, IL: Research Press.

Horne, A. M., Orpinas, P., Newman-Carlson, D., & Bartolomucci, C. (2004). Elementary school Bully Busters program: Understanding why children bully and what to do about it. In D. L. Espelage & S. M. Swearer (Eds.), *Bullying in American schools: A social-ecological perspective on prevention and intervention* (pp. 297–325). Mahwah, NJ: Lawrence Erlbaum.

Institute of Medicine. (2001). *Crossing the quality chasm: A new health system for the 21st century.* Washington, DC: National Academy Press.

Kellam, S. G., & Van Horn, Y. V. (1997). Life course development, community epidemiology, and preventive trials: A scientific structure for prevention research. *American Journal of Community Psychology, 25,* 177–188.

Kenny, M., Waldo, M., Warter, E., & Barton, C. (2002). Theory, science, and practice for enhancing the lives of children and youth. *The Counseling Psychologist, 30,* 726–748.

Limber, S. (2004). Implementation of the Olweus bullying prevention program in American schools: Lessons learned from the field. In D. L. Espelage & S. M. Swearer (Eds.), *Bullying in American schools: A social-ecological perspective on prevention and intervention* (pp. 351–363). Mahwah, NJ: Lawrence Erlbaum.

Messer, S. B. (2004). Evidence-based practice: Beyond empirically supported treatments. *Professional Psychology: Research and Practice, 35,* 580–588. doi:10.1037/-735-7028.35.6.580

Mishna, F., Khoury-Kassabri, M., Gadalla, T., & Daciuk, J. (2012). Risk factors for involvement in cyber bullying: Victims, bullies and bully-victims. *Children and Youth Services Review, 34*(1), 63–70.

Nation, M., Crusto, C., Wandersman, A., Kumpfer, K. L., Seybolt, D., Morrissey-Kane, E., & Davino, K. (2003). What works in prevention: Principles of effective prevention programs. *American Psychologist, 58,* 449–456. doi:10.1037/0003-066X.58.6-7.449

National Institute of Mental Health. (1998). *Priorities for prevention research at NIMH: A report by the national advisory mental health council workgroup on mental disorder prevention research* (NIH Publication No. 98-4321). Bethesda, MD: Author.

Newsome, S., Waldo, M., & Gruszka, C. (2012). Mindfulness group work: Preventing stress and increasing self-compassion among helping professionals in training. *Journal for Specialists in Group Work.* Advance online publication. doi:10.1080/01933922.2012.690832

Norcross, J. C., Beutler, E. L., & Levant, R. F. (2006). *Evidence-based practices in mental health.* Washington, DC: American Psychological Association.

O'Connell, M. E., Boat, T., & Warner, K. E. (Eds.). (2009). *Preventing mental, emotional, and behavioral disorders among young people: Progress and possibilities.* Washington, DC: National Academies Press.

Orpinas, P., & Horne, A. H. (2006). *Bullying prevention: Creating a positive school climate and developing social competence.* Washington, DC: American Psychological Association.

Park, C. L., Aldwin, C. M., Fenster, J. R., & Snyder, L. B. (2008). Pathways to post-traumatic growth versus posttraumatic stress: Coping and emotional reactions following the September 11, 2001, terrorist attacks. *American Journal of Orthopsychiatry, 78*(3), 300–312.

Patton, M. (2002). *Qualitative research and evaluation methods.* Thousand Oaks, CA: Sage.

Petrosino, A., Turpin-Petrosino, C., & Finckenauer, J. O. (2000). Well-meaning programs can have harmful effects! Lessons from experiments of programs such as Scared Straight. *Crime & Delinquency, 46*(3), 354–379. doi:10.1177/0011128700046003006

Ponterotto, J. G. (2005). Qualitative research in counseling psychology: A Primer on Research Paradigms and Philosophy of Science. *Journal of Counseling Psychology, 52*(2), 126–136.

Poulsen, M. N., Vandenhoudt, H., Wyckoff, S. C., Obong'o, C. O., Ochura, J., Njika, G., . . . Miller, K. S. (2010). Cultural adaptation of a U.S. evidence-based parenting intervention for rural western Kenya: From Parents Matter! to Families Matter! *AIDS Education and Prevention, 22*(4), 273–285.

Raines, J. C. (2008). *Evidence-based practice in school mental health.* New York, NY: Oxford University Press.

Rieckmann, T., Bergmann, L., & Rasplica, C. (2011). Legislating clinical practice: Counselor responses to an evidence-based practice mandate. *Journal of Psychoactive Drugs, 43,* 27–39. doi:10.1080/02791072.2011.601988

Rigby, K. (2009). School bullying and the case for the method of shared concern. In S. Jimerson, S. Swearer, & D. Espelage (Eds.), *The international handbook of school bullying* (pp. 547–558). New York, NY: Routledge.

Romano, J., & Hage, S. (2000). Prevention: A call to action. *The Counseling Psychologist, 28,* 854–856.

Sackett, D. L., Straus, S. E., Richardson, W. S., Rosenberg, W., & Haynes R. B. (2000). *Evidence-based medicine: How to practice and teach EBM* (2nd ed.). London, England: Churchill Livingstone.

Schwartz, J., & Waldo, M. (1999). Therapeutic factors in spouse abuse treatment. *Journal for Specialists in Group Work, 24,* 197–207.

Schwartz, J., & Waldo, M. (2003). Reducing gender role conflict among men attending partner abuse prevention groups. *Journal for Specialists in Group Work, 28,* 355–369.

Sue, S., & Zane, N. (2006). Ethnic minority populations have been neglected by evidence-based practices. In J. C. Norcross, L. E. Beutler, & R. F. Levant (Eds.), *Evidence-based practices in mental health: Debate and dialogue on the fundamental questions* (pp. 329–337). Washington, DC: American Psychological Association.

Sullivan, H. S. (1938). Psychiatry: Introduction to the study of interpersonal relations. *Psychiatry, 1,* 121–134.

Ttofi, M. M., & Farrington, D. P. (2011). Effectiveness of school-based programs to reduce bullying: A systematic and meta-analytic review. *Journal of Experimental Criminology, 7,* 27–56.

Twain, M. (2006). Chapters from my autobiography. *New American Review, 598.* Retrieved from http://www.gutenberg.org/files/19987/19987.txt. (Original work published 1906)

Waldo, M. (1984). Roommate communication as related to students' personal and social adjustment. *Journal of College Student Personnel, 25,* 39–44.

Waldo, M. (1985). Improving Interpersonal communication in a university residential community. *Journal of Humanistic Education and Development, 23,* 126–133.

Waldo, M. (1986a). Academic achievement and retention as related to students' personal and social adjustment. *Journal of College and University Student Housing, 16,* 19–23.

Waldo, M. (1986b). Group counseling for military personnel who battered their wives. *Journal for Specialists in Group Work, 11,* 132–138.

Waldo, M. (1987). Also victims: Understanding and treating men arrested for spouse abuse. *Journal of Counseling and Development, 65,* 385–388.

Waldo, M. (1988). Relationship enhancement counseling groups for wife abusers. *Journal of Mental Health Counseling, 10,* 37–45.

Waldo, M. (1989). Primary prevention in university residence halls: Paraprofessional led relationship enhancement groups for college roommates. *Journal of Counseling and Development, 67,* 465–471.

Waldo, M., & Fuhriman, A. (1981). Roommate relationships, communication skills, and psychological adjustment in residence halls. *Journal of College and University Student Housing, 11,* 31–35.

Waldo, M., & Harman, M. J. (1999). Relationship enhancement groups with state hospital patients and staff. *Journal for Specialists in Group Work, 24,* 27–36.

Waldo, M., Kerne, P., & Van Horne Kerne, V. (2007). Therapeutic factors in guidance/psycho-educational versus counseling/interpersonal problem solving sessions in domestic violence intervention groups. *Journal for Specialists in Group Work, 32,* 346–361.

Waldo, M., & Morrill, W. (1983). Roommate communication skills workshops in university residence halls. *Journal of College and University Student Housing, 13,* 31–36.

Waldo, M., & Schwartz, J. P. (2003). *Research competencies in prevention.* Presentation in the symposium "Prevention Competencies" at the American Psychological Association, Toronto, Ontario, Canada.

West, S. L., & O'Neal, K. K. (2004). Project D.A.R.E. Outcome Effectiveness Revisited. *American Journal of Public Health, 94,* 1027–1029.

Westen, D. I. (2006). Patients and treatments in clinical trials are not adequately representative of clinical practices. In J. C. Norcross, L. E. Beutler, & R. F. Levant (Eds.), *Evidence-based practices in mental health: Debate and dialogue on the fundamental questions* (pp. 161–171). Washington, DC: American Psychological Association.

Index

About the Authors _____

Katherine Raczynski, PhD, is a graduate of the Department of Educational Psychology and Instructional Technology in the College of Education at the University of Georgia where she earned a PhD in educational psychology. She has worked in the field of adolescent violence prevention as part of the Healthy Teens program and the Multisite Violence Prevention Project, a 7-year series of studies investigating students' social development as they transition from middle school to high school. She has also worked with students, teachers, and parents to reduce bullying and aggression in schools as part of the Bully Busters program, and she is coauthor of three forthcoming books in the Bully Busters publication series. Katherine is the recipient of the 2009 APA Society of Counseling Psychology Prevention Section Graduate Student Prevention Research Award and Research Proposal Award, the 2010 APA Division 16 School Psychology Award for Outstanding Student Scholarship, and she was named a 2011 David Watts Scholar by the Southeast Regional Association of Teacher Educators. In her free time, she enjoys cooking, traveling, reading, and spending time with family.

Michael Waldo, PhD, is a psychologist and professor with the Department of Counseling and Educational Psychology at New Mexico State University. He is a Fellow in the American Psychological Association, chairs the "Prevention in Counseling Psychology" editorial board, and is a past chair of the Society of Counseling Psychology's Prevention Section. His research and practice have focused on preventing problems and fostering development through promotion of positive interpersonal relationships. He has published 40 plus manuscripts addressing prevention, including studies of problem epidemiology; evaluations of primary, secondary, and tertiary preventive interventions; and descriptions of prevention service delivery systems. His work in prevention has resulted in his receiving eight national awards, including the Lifetime Achievement Award in Prevention.

Jonathan P. Schwartz, PhD, is a professor and department head in the Department of Counseling and Educational Psychology at New Mexico State University. He is the past chair of the Division 17 Prevention Section and executive board member of the Council of Counseling Psychology Training Programs. Dr. Schwartz has published in the area of men and masculinity, prevention, and intimate violence. He was awarded the 2008 Researcher of the Year Award from Division 51 (Psychological Study of Men and Masculinity) of the American Psychological Association and received the 2011 Fritz and Linn Kuder Early Career Scientist/Practitioner Award from the American Psychologist Association Division of Counseling Psychology.

Arthur M. Horne, PhD, Dean of Education and Distinguished Research Professor Emeritus at the University of Georgia, is a licensed psychologist and is a Fellow of the Association for Specialists in Group Work (ASGW) and the American Psychological Association, as well as several divisions of APA. He has more than 40 years of professional experience as a university professor, department head, program coordinator for counseling psychology and for marriage and family therapy programs, and as a consultant and trainer. Andy has received recognition for his work, including the American Psychological Association's Society of Counseling Psychology Awards for Social Justice, Psychology Faces of Counseling Psychology, and the Lifetime Achievement Award in Prevention. He has received the Extended Research Award from the American Counseling Association, the Eminent Career Award from the ASGW, Distinguished Alumni Award from Southern Illinois University, and has served as a Soros Open Society International Scholar. He was president of the APA's Division of Group Psychology and Group Psychotherapy and also of the ACA's Association for Specialists in Group Work. He is president-elect of the APA Division 17, Society of Counseling Psychology. He has more than 200 scholarly publications and presentations including 9 coauthored and 5 coedited books in his areas of expertise (group work, prevention, bullying and violence reduction, and marriage and family counseling), along with broad international consultation in these areas. Andy and his wife take pleasure in travels, and particularly enjoy spending time on the Oregon coast to enjoy the ocean, mountains, rivers, and abundance of nature.

⑤SAGE research**methods**

The essential online tool for researchers from the world's leading methods publisher

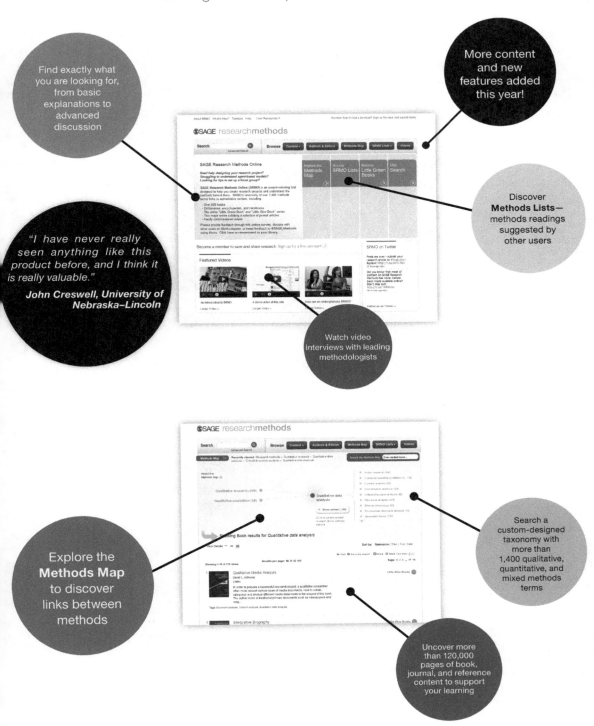

Find exactly what you are looking for, from basic explanations to advanced discussion

More content and new features added this year!

"I have never really seen anything like this product before, and I think it is really valuable."

John Creswell, University of Nebraska–Lincoln

Discover **Methods Lists**— methods readings suggested by other users

Watch video interviews with leading methodologists

Explore the **Methods Map** to discover links between methods

Search a custom-designed taxonomy with more than 1,400 qualitative, quantitative, and mixed methods terms

Uncover more than 120,000 pages of book, journal, and reference content to support your learning

Find out more at
www.sageresearchmethods.com